How to Read With Your Children

Parent/Caregiver's Guide

by Phyllis A. Wilken

SOPRIS
WEST

4093 Specialty Place   ◆   Longmont, CO 80504   ◆   (303) 651-2829
www.sopriswest.com

Dedication

I dedicate this book to family reading and to my family which spans four generations. This family photo represents three generations. We all enjoy reading together and individually and have great, long discussions about what we have read.

The four women in the photo have a combined

Royce Wilken, Delmar Wilken, Lyndell Wilken, Kent Hunter
Tyler Wilken, Lois Wilken, Phyllis Wilken, Mylla Wilken Hunter, Zachary Wilken

total of 75 years of teaching experience. Lyndell has taught grades 1-12, and is presently teaching at Lane Community College in Eugene, Oregon. Lois taught grades 1-6 in Nebraska, near Omaha. She is now a stay-at-home parent and volunteers many hours in Ellisville Elementary and Crestwood Middle School in Missouri, is a Scout Leader, and is a church and Vacation Bible School teacher and coordinator. Mylla taught first grade in Houston, Texas and third grade at Palos Park, Illinois. She has been an assistant principal there, and is presently serving as the coordinator of the district's Emergent Literacy Program.

The men are avid readers too! Royce works for Archer Daniels Midland (ADM) in St. Louis, Kent is a self-employed communications consultant, and my husband is professor emeritus of agricultural economics at the University of Illinois. Thanks to him for putting this book on the word processor.

Our two grandsons, Tyler and Zachary, love reading! When they visit it is my great privilege to read special books to them—the books I read to our children! Those books are their favorites and they still occupy a special place in our house and always will.

My mother, Kathryn Anderson, is not pictured here. But I owe my creativity and my love for reading to her. As a mother of seven children, she did not have much time for reading to us. However, Sunday evenings were devoted to family activities led by my mother. She would draw cartoons and together we would make up appropriate stories for them. That activity was followed by reading a Bible story and then another story. It was a time of learning about my mother's values and beliefs, and my brothers' and sisters' interests and opinions. It was a special time in my life. So my family reading experiences span four generations! I wish all children had that kind of mother.

This book is also dedicated to all parents and caregivers who will be motivated to read with their children because they read this guide. If you have not started reading with your children or grandchildren, do so now. Remember, you are your children's first, favorite, and most influential teacher. You are not only reading to and for them, but also their children and their grandchildren. Love of reading and the value derived from it carries over from generation to generation.

Acknowledgments

I am grateful to our daughter, Mylla Wilken Hunter, a former reading teacher, assistant principal, and now director of the Emergent Literacy Program for the Palos Park, Illinois School District for reviewing every word on every page. Her knowledge of reading and suggestions for the guide made the task of writing this easier.

I wish to thank the following people: Dr. Carolyn Farrar, manager, and Robert Rush, principal consultant of the Intervention and Improvement section of Chapter 1, Illinois State Board of Education, who funded the project "What To Do When You Read With Children," which provided the content for this guide; Jane Quinlan, Illinois Regional Office of Education, who administered the grant; Jean Osborn, associate director of the Center for the Study of Reading, who directed this study and encouraged me to write this guide; Dr. Judith Barbour who wrote the literature review and analysis and the Foreword; Terry Denny, professor emeritus, Educational Psychology, University of Illinois, who was an expert in the interpretation and analysis of the results; and the 241 people who completed the questionnaires.

About the Author

Phyllis A. Wilken began her 50-year career as an educator in a one-room school house in Cullom, Illinois teaching grades 1-8. She became a curriculum coordinator, then an acting middle school assistant principal before becoming the principal at Garden Hills Elementary School in Champaign, Illinois. Her own experiences first as a teacher, then as a parent, and finally as an administrator showed her the importance of paying attention to individual children's needs. She guided Garden Hills on an improvement mission that resulted in the school receiving the United States Department of Education's Blue Ribbon Award for Excellence in Elementary Education.

From 1945, in a Cullom, Illinois one-room rural school to Champaign, Illinois Garden Hills Elementary School's Blue Ribbon Award for Excellence, Phyllis A. Wilken shares her experience and enthusiasm for creating excellence in education by involving parents/caregivers and making them partners in their children's learning.

Since her retirement in 1987 she has served as a educational consultant for the University of Illinois, College of Education, Center for the Study of Reading. She worked with E.D. Hirsch, author of *Cultural Literacy*, on the development of the six books *What Your 1st-6th Grader Needs to Know* and *A First Dictionary of Cultural Literacy*. She has served on many boards and committees, including, from 1990-1994, the U.S. Office of Education review panel that selected the National Diffusion Network model reading programs and the Blue Ribbon Elementary Schools, as well as the Illinois State Board of Education Retired Administrative Services Committee.

She received the National Association of Direct Instruction Award for Administrators, the Outstanding Educator Award conferred by the YWCA, and the Illinois Regional Office of Education Award. She is listed in *Who's Who of American Women* and *Outstanding Elementary Teachers in America*. She currently is the president of the University of Illinois College of Education Alumni Board, and has received the University of Illinois College of Education Outstanding Alumni Award.

She is also the author of a book about Garden Hills Elementary School's journey to excellence entitled *Turning Our School Around: Seven Common-sense Steps to School Improvement.*

Foreword

To a great extent, language and reading foundations are developed in the home before children ever reach school age. Children base their language learning on the practical problem-solving activities of everyday life starting at birth. What happens in the home is critically important to the attitudes, behaviors, and skills that a child will develop; and these attitudes, behaviors, and skills lay the groundwork for what the child will be doing in school. They will determine, to a large degree, how successful the child will be in the development of reading skills.

Parents play the greatest role in setting the language learning pattern for their children. A parent's attitude and behaviors displayed to the child during the child's early years can either be beneficial to later school success and reading ability, or they can be detrimental. Parents' positive attitudes about reading and frequent use of books will usually produce positive attitudes and reading success in their children. However, that alone is not enough; the more successful readers are those who have actually been read to by their parents or caregivers. Parents can help set a beneficial language learning and reading pattern for their children by making reading aloud with their children a natural and enjoyable part of family life.

Helping parents set these patterns is the very focus of this book. Many parents realize the importance of reading with their children, but somehow they do not find the way to make it happen. If you are a parent who finds this to be true in your family life, you are not alone. But there is a solution. The simple suggestions presented in this book can be used by any adult. The techniques offered have been shown to improve the attitudes and skills of the children presented with them. Furthermore, they are sure to provide enjoyment and delight for both children and parents.

I became acquainted with Phyllis Wilken through our association at the University of Illinois, and over the years we have collaborated on numerous research and teaching projects. I know Phyllis to be extremely well-informed of the difficulties parents face while trying to offer their children the best learning environment possible. Phyllis Wilken has worked closely with hundreds of families and has come to know firsthand their trials, time constraints, fears, and desires for their children's future success. She became aware of the need to offer simple strategies and techniques that would help parents find a way to bring to their children the very important experience of being read to. I applaud her efforts and have seen the positive results.

You will enjoy this book as well as learn from it. And better still, your child will benefit. Children want to be read to, and although parents usually realize the importance of this activity and want to read aloud to their children, the realities of everyday life often present obstacles. In this book, Phyllis Wilken brings to all parents and caregivers a way to make it happen.

Judith A. Barbour, Ph.D.

Table of Contents

Section One

Introduction

The Importance of Reading With Your Child

When my teaching career began in a K-8, one-room, rural school in central Illinois in 1944, parents were intrinsically involved in every facet of the school's operation. Those parents accepted as a fact that their children would learn to read, write, and compute. They expected their children to achieve in a continuous fashion throughout the eight years that they attended the rural school. When the children did not achieve or progress as expected, the parents were the first to offer their help and assistance. This kind of parental interest and involvement developed within children a belief that learning and school were important, and that learning was a responsibility that the students and their parents cooperatively shared with the teachers.

The verbal and nonverbal communications in the family at that time served many purposes. Children could develop their language skills through the continuous interactions that occurred with adults, siblings, and peers without the competition and interruptions from television, the telephone, and radio. The children learned to listen and to follow instructions while learning their household and farm duties. They were expected to begin, carry out, and finish tasks in an efficient and responsible manner. The finished task or product was expected to be done well, and feedback (positive or negative) was immediately and diligently given by adults or older siblings. Many of these activities that children engaged in were prerequisites for the task of learning to read.

In most rural and urban homes until the late 1930s or early 1940s, the children's help was needed to operate an efficient household. In addition, most parents assumed it was their responsibility to teach their children the basics of living. In other words, they were taught because people's lifestyle, culture, and their child rearing practices required it. In addition, respect for adults, the parents, and particularly the teacher was assumed by students. Children in these families learned about being a part of a self-sufficient group, cooperatively working with one another to complete a task. In this process, they usually developed a good self-concept and had confidence in their ability to contribute to the group. They had pride in the achievement and accomplishments of their daily tasks.

In our society today, child rearing and parenting have changed dramatically. It has always been evolving and changing, but a major shift came in the United States before, during, and after World War II. A few women worked during the Depression years, but many of them did this work in their home. During the war years many mothers, grandmothers, aunts, and neighborhood women, who had usually been in the home, went to work in the industries and assembly plants. Not all of them returned, in post-World War II America, to the job of full-time homemaker. As time went on, increasing numbers of parents left the home and entered the work force. With the absence of both parents from the home, inadvertently the preparation of young children for learning in school slowly diminished and declined. In today's economy, very few families can afford the luxury of having a parent care for young children at home.

Added to the working-parent phenomenon is the increase in the number of one-parent families. The fact is that child rearing is a difficult, demanding task that is ideally accomplished by a caring mother and father when and wherever possible. Yet it is a fortunate family indeed in which the father is closely involved in the daily care, nurturing, and rearing of the children; assists with the household chores and meal preparation; communicates with the school and teachers on everything from school activities to his child's performance; and helps to provide what is needed during school hours to improve the education of his children.

Even when the nuclear family holds fast, a third concern is the mobility and transiency of both the nuclear and extended families, and the neighborhoods. Many times grandparents live far away where it is warm in the winter and another place that is cool in the summer. Such grandparents cannot provide the continuous, loving child care and educationally influence their grandchildren when parents are working or are absent from the home. In pre-World War II times, neighborhood families helped to look after one another's children and surveyed the neighborhood constantly to see if the children were safe and close by. In today's world we sometimes do not even know our next-door and across-the-street neighbors! Yet we hope they will be kind to our children and not verbally, physically, or sexually abuse them.

Finally, a technological revolution has occurred in our society that has adversely affected and changed parent/child relationships and the development of children. That technology has produced television, VCRs, telephones and cellular phones, computers and global connections, etc. While these innovations may be good for business, they now absorb much of the time that families used to spend in conversation about the usual "going-ons"; playing games; reading to their children or having children read to their parents; carrying out family chores or tasks; and taking an active interest in and supporting learning through family conversations about educational activities and events. Plus fast and frozen foods have shortened family meals, which leaves less time for family interactions.

Working parents, the single parent, mobility, and technology are changes to which we must adjust. I, for one, would not want to return to a world without the mobility, technology, or equal employment opportunities of today. But we do have to identify the problems that these societal changes have spawned in our homes and our families. Parents today face a more complicated set of difficult challenges. Yet we must find ways to compensate for the losses in the development of our young children.

Society's answer has been to provide daycare programs for preschool children. They are a help in solving some of the problems. But, I believe, such endeavors alone are not enough. There is a need to go beyond providing preschool facilities for children. There is a need to focus on the home. There is a need to enable all parents—whether working, single, or without the support of their extended family—to provide experiences that will later help their children to learn at school.

There is a need to recapture some of the helpful prereading experiences in which families were involved in the past. While it will by no means solve all society's ills, I believe that reading with young children is a first step. When parents/caregivers can read with their own children for even a ten-minute period five times per week, this enables the parents/caregivers to enhance, enrich, and extend their children's learning. In this way, they indeed can become their children's first, most influential, and favorite teachers.

Reading is an important skill for children to learn in the early, or primary, years in school. It is important because it forms and builds the foundation for all future learning. Reading holds the key to expanding your child's interests in and understanding of the world both close to her/him and far away, as well as communicating with the people who inhabit the world.

Reading with your child, starting at birth, acquaints him/her with books and print. It builds a bank of knowledge which builds interest and enjoyment of places that your child may visit as an adult, or may never visit in person. It expands your child's interest in many different areas, such as art, music, history, science, and sports. Your child acquires this knowledge by your reading and talking with him/her about these areas. This, in turn, encourages and motivates your child to want to read and learn on his/her own.

If your child has not been prepared in this way, she/he will be behind children who have had this experience when your child enters school. The teacher then has to teach the children those things that could have been taught in the home. The teacher cannot begin the teaching of reading to your child, and the other children in the class, unless the parents/caregivers have done their job in the home. The research that supports these assertions is discussed in detail in Appendix I, for those who are interested.

Why Many Parents/Caregivers Don't Read to Their Children

Reading with their children is an easy way for parents/caregivers to prepare, help, and motivate their children to want to learn to read and/or to become better readers. Yet many parents/caregivers don't make reading with their children a priority. Why is this so? An interesting study[*] was conducted in 1989 to answer that question. The five most common responses that parents gave as reasons for not reading aloud to their children were these:

1. "I couldn't do that. I'm no good at speaking/reading literature/telling stories."

2. "I can't afford the time or money to read to my child as much as I'd like."

3. "The child I care about is too young (or too old) to be read to."

4. "I don't see how I can make reading out loud compete with TV."

5. "It won't do much good anyway."

Obviously you have some interest in reading with your child, or you wouldn't be reading this book. But if you agreed with any of the five responses, and are not yet convinced of the need to read with your child

---

[*] Craig & Roth (1989). In D.S. Strickland and L.M. Morrow (Eds.), *Emerging literacy: Young children learn to read and write* (pp. 33-35). Newark, NJ: International Reading Association.

one a regular basis, read on. Let's consider these five problems in another way, and how you might solve them for the benefit of your child.

◆ **"I couldn't do that. I'm no good at speaking/ reading literature/ telling stories."**

Parents/caregivers should focus on the fact that just the act of reading demonstrates to children that parents believe reading is important. It shapes children's attitudes toward reading. Remember, young children really do not know or care how well you read, but what your child will remember is the pleasant time you had together, the attention she/he received from you, and the enjoyment of talking about a story and sharing your beliefs and values through reading stories.

◆ **"I can't afford the time or money to read to my child as much as I'd like."**

Most parents/caregivers have access to public and school libraries. They do not need to spend money for books. Exchanging books with neighbors, friends, and relatives is also possible. Garage sales, used book stores, and paperback book sales at school are economical places to purchases books.

Time is a factor, but you must find time to read! I suggest that you read for a minimum of ten minutes per day, five days per week. That amounts to 50 minutes per week—less than an hour. How many minutes per week do you and your child spend watching television? I expect if you are similar to the average American family, it amounts to an hour or more per day. You should be willing to spend 50 minutes per week reading with and to your child. This time commitment is little and the benefits are many.

In addition, the time a family spends personally communicating with one another about a story during reading time will provide enjoyable moments and memories for your child for the present as well as for the rest of his/her life. Talking, laughing, or being sad about a story establishes and develops communication among family members that lasts a lifetime.

◆ **"The child I care about is too young (or too old) to be read to."**

Your child is never too young or too old to be read to. This is a practice that lasts a lifetime. It leads to sharing what you read with family members all your life. I am constantly reading to my husband and he to me items from books, magazines, and newspapers that we know would be of interest to one another, or items of common interest. We constantly clip articles and send them to our adult children and their families. This habit of sharing started when we read together when they were children. We still buy books for them. But we only know what to buy today by having read to them and by noting their interests.

If we had not read with them and to one another from infancy to adulthood we would not be able to follow the general and reading interests of our family. The quality of your family relationships can be developed and enhanced through reading at any age. We as adults are never too old or too young to be read to, but your child especially is never too old or too young for reading with you.

◆ **"I don't see how I can make reading out loud compete with TV."**

You are not competing with television. Watching television and reading with your child are two very different activities. Television is passive and reading is interactive. Television does not allow for the kind of discussion that reading generates. Children seldom ask problem-solving questions or the definitions of words during a television program. There is little or no review or reflection, and little discussion of the values or beliefs embodied in the television program. Why is this true? Because for many families there is the next program and/or the next advertisement to watch, which results in another hour of passive entertainment with little or no thinking, predicting, problem solving, forming of opinions, following the development of a story, and little association with print, letters, and words. Reading embodies all of those things plus giving your undivided attention for ten minutes per day to your child.

◆ **"It won't do much good anyway."**

Parents/caregivers should never underestimate the good that reading with and to their children can do. If parents/caregivers do not read the language or do not feel competent to read to their children, there is a host of activities they can do that will impart to their children that they believe learning to read and being the best reader possible is important. Those activities are discussed later in this book, and provide parents/caregivers with many options for participating in the process of teaching their children to become the best reader possible. Remember that you are your child's first teacher and her/his most influential one. Believe that this is true and begin reading with and to your child. It makes a difference in how your child will perform in school and for a lifetime.

How This Simple Program Can Help

I recommend that parents (and/or other caregivers) read with their children ten minutes daily, five days per week. Why? Because it is "doable." It is a realistic expectation for working parents and single parent families given the time constraints in our fast-paced daily lives and schedules.

When it is possible for parents/caregivers to read for more than ten minutes, that is wonderful! Sometimes reading to several of your children at one time is another way to be able to read for more than ten minutes with all your children. The idea, however, is to read to each child individually most of the time. This assures that the side benefits of reading, such as the undivided attention that a parent bestows on a child, gives you an opportunity to observe and note what your child's favorite stories and interests are and to learn how you can expand those interests. It also provides you with an opportunity to focus on the ways in which your child's knowledge is growing and developing.

It is important that the ten-minute period becomes a significant, structured activity in your family schedule. It should take precedence over other duties or desires on the part of both parents/caregivers and children. To ensure that this time commitment for reading is carried out, parents/caregivers and the children should keep a written record of their weekly reading. Perhaps they can cross out the dates on which they read each week on each child's calendar. Or they can create a family schedule for each week and record the five days that they read. This schedule could be displayed on the refrigerator with a magnet, for example. If so, it should be placed at your child's eye level so she/he can do her/his own recording.

By keeping a record you are making a strong statement to your child that you believe reading is important and that you value reading. You are demonstrating to your child that reading with him/her is your favorite time also, as you nurture your child and make positive statements about his/her interests and provide answers to his/her questions. You should also express your appreciation for the time you have together. By reading with your child, you share your values and beliefs as you comment on the "moral of the story" and the characters in the story.

In the course of each week, you will be able to observe your child's reading development and performance. This will give you a "common ground" on which to discuss with your child's teacher (if your child is school age) your child's progress or lack of it. Then you can intelligently discuss, through your own discoveries and the teacher's suggestions, how you might fully participate in the responsibility of making your child a lifelong, independent reader. Isn't this worth spending ten minutes per day reading with each of your children?

I must share with you two of my real life school experiences. As a K-6 elementary principal of the Garden Hills Elementary School in Champaign, Illinois, I was asked to serve as a consultant for one of the most outstanding reports on reading produced in our nation. This report, titled "Becoming A Nation of Readers," was by the Commission on Reading, which included the National Academy of Education, the National Institute of Education, and the Center for the Study of Reading at the University of Illinois. This report is filled with common sense facts, information, and research findings on reading. It is written in a friendly style and language that parents can understand. I suggest that parents order this book. (Contact the Center for the Study of Reading, University of Illinois, 158 CRC, 51 Gerty Drive, Champaign, Illinois 61821.)

There are many profound, memorable statements in this report. It states that reading begins in the home. Children learn by their parents/caregivers reading aloud to them from birth on, and by talking with them about books (such as identifying the pictures) and ultimately encouraging them to think, to solve problems, and to make decisions through questions when reading. This stimulates children's intellectual growth and prepares and motivates them to want to learn to read and to become skilled readers. As summarized on page 23 on the report: "The single most important activity for building the knowledge required for eventual success in reading is reading aloud to children."

The other experience is what happened at Garden Hills Elementary School when the teaching staff and I developed a Garden Hills Family Reading Club for our school of approximately 550 children. By focusing on reading at school, we had already improved the average reading performance of our students at each grade level by three to six months. This was quite an accomplishment in a school with many special needs children and a 40% transient rate per year. It was rewarding to have children who had never experienced success in reading before ask us, "When are we going to have reading?" They demonstrated a joy and enthusiasm for reading that I had never experienced in all my years of teaching since 1945. They became confident readers, willing to accept tasks that we thought might be too difficult for them, and asked for more words to read.

As a staff, we all came to the conclusion that we must involve the children's parents! Why? There was never enough time in the school day for the children to practice their reading skills by reading aloud, and no one except the single teacher to motivate each child in the classroom to continue their learning. The parents were the logical people to turn to. We feared that many of the parents might not want to become involved, as many of them came from unfortunate childhood circumstances and had not experienced success in school themselves. But we had encountered many an obstacle to learning before, as our school journeyed to excellence and the Rose Garden at the White House in Washington, D.C. to receive our Blue Ribbon Award for Excellence in Elementary Education in 1986.

One thing we knew for certain. We had to be realistic in recommending the amount of time we suggested to the parents to read with their children. After all, many of them had never read to or with their children before, and many others had limited time to do so. We decided that ten minutes per day five days per week was a realistic expectation, and the parents agreed. Those parents read approximately 3,000 hours total the first year, and doubled the hours the second year! The students' improved reading performance continued for as long as I was principal. The parents diligently read to and with their children, and were excited by the results.

We even experienced three days of filming for a nationally televised, hour-long documentary called "Drop Everything and Read (DEAR)," along with two other public schools in the United States, about our outstanding family reading club. It was televised on the three major networks and by a public broadcasting company. Two of our school's families were featured reading to their children at home. It was a proud moment for our staff, students, and their families! Information about the club is included in Appendix II if you are interested in learning more about it. The Reading Partners program, in which Garden Hills Elementary School involved senior citizens, community members, and parents is discussed in Appendix III.

My purpose in telling you this experience is that I know what a tremendous influence parents and children reading together can have on children's learning in and out of school. It is amazing that a ten-minute reading period five times per week, for a mere total of 50 minutes per week, can have this kind of impact. I know that this commitment to reading can happen in your home as it did in the homes of the students at Garden Hills Elementary School. Both you and your child will be glad and fulfilled because you have read together! It will maximize learning for your child.

This guide is filled with suggestions, activities, and ideas to enable parents/caregivers to fulfill this responsibility of reading to and with their children. Enjoy . . . and pleasant reading!

Summary Box

♦ *Read to your child for ten minutes daily, five days per week.*

♦ *If you have more than one child, try to read to each child individually as much as possible, with a family reading time once per week.*

♦ *Keep a record of each child's reading times.*

♦ *Enjoy this special time, and let your child know that you do!*

♦ *Notice your child's progress and reading performance.*

The Wilken Family Reading Schedule
(Check the days you read with Mom or Dad.)

Children	S	M	T	W	Th	F	S
Lyndell	✓	✓		✓		✓	✓
Royce	✓		✓	✓		✓	
Mylla	✓		✓	✓		✓	✓

(Note that the children never went more than one day in a row without reading.)

Section Two

Reading With Your Child

Following are introductions to eight topics which provide answers to questions commonly asked by parents/caregivers about reading with children.

After each introduction is a list of common sense activities and suggestions that will be useful to you. They require little time and minimal resources. They will make a difference in your child's attitude, achievement, and interest in reading.

Why Read to Your Child?

Many parents/caregivers read to their children because they believe it is an enjoyable family activity. This is the most important reason, but there are many other reasons why parents/caregivers should read to their children. If more parents knew that social needs, such as nurturing, loving, and approving of their children's actions could be satisfied in a ten-minute reading session, they might be convinced that reading daily with their children is one of the most important activities of child rearing. Academic needs may also be satisfied. Together they can influence the development of a secure child with an inquiring mind.

What is a social need? Your child grows in many ways and one of these ways is becoming a socially acceptable person who values others, and responds to them in an emotional way that is appropriate. Many examples of this kind of person are found in children's literature and books. Reading and discussing stories with all kinds of characters and their emotions that may or may not meet your approval helps you to teach your child what kind of person you want her/him to be. Some of the emotions that one encounters and responds to when reading are joy, disappointment, fear, sadness, pleasure, and others. Reading together offers an opportunity for a family to share these emotions. Your child can learn from you how to react emotionally to various situations by sharing and discussing what you read together. These family discussions provide an opportunity for you to build a foundation for the development of an emotionally stable and secure child who has learned from you how to react and respond to emotions in an appropriate way.

I am reminded of our oldest daughter Lyndell, who at two and one-half years of age loved the story *Goldilocks and The Three Bears*. However, she always cried "crocodile tears" when we came to the part in the story where Goldilocks ate all of Baby Bear's porridge. Through our discussion of this often read story, our two year old learned that some stories are make believe, that it was alright to cry about this situation, and that Goldilocks should not have entered someone else's home and eaten their food. As your child responds to stories in a similar manner and asks questions and draws conclusions about happenings in a story, she/he is developing an emotional stability for use when similar situations occur in real life later. You have an opportunity and responsibility to shape and mold your child's social and moral character. When you do, your child may be influenced to behave in a manner that you deem proper and responsible.

Through reading together, these family values and attitudes are formed for your child, and probably for the future generations of your family. When your child grows up and possibly becomes a parent, she/he will pass on to her/his children the desirable habits, practices, and values that you taught, such as reading in the family. As an adult, your child's family may also use family reading, as you did, to transfer your family's values. This practice, which is passed from one generation to the next, prepares your child for living in a peaceful manner in a secure and stable family. In this way, you the parent/caregiver become your child's most influential teacher.

For example, our children would often tell us what other children in the neighborhood and at school would do and say which they thought was inappropriate (according to our family's standards). One time our son asked another child, "Didn't your mom and dad tell you that was bad? You should not do that. That was not nice to talk to her that way." When that child went into his house and told his mother what Royce had said to him, she came outside and told Royce to leave their property. She said it was none of Royce's business what she told her kids. Such behavior on the part of this parent told Royce that their value system was different than our family's. It appeared that in that family there probably was little imparting of values through family reading and discussions.

We also read to satisfy a child's academic needs. What is an academic need? This need requires us to enlarge and expand the information and knowledge that your child possesses which provides her/him with the proper background for learning to read. This knowledge brings an understanding of the printed word. Because you have provided this background, your child will later be motivated to read in areas that she/he is not familiar with, such as performing arts, science, technology, different cultures and races, and the information projected on her/his personal computer screen either at home or at school.

Parents/caregivers also have needs that they wish to fulfill. First and foremost they want to be good parents, to guide their children's moral, social, and academic development, and to feel proud of the efforts and progress they are making. They need to enjoy their family as they raise secure and stable children who can make a contribution to society as adults. A daily ten-minute reading session can help parents/caregivers to satisfy their own needs as well as their children's social and academic needs.

Why

Read to Your Child?

◆ **Social Reasons**

Reading to your child . . .

- Provides enjoyment, fun, and entertainment.
- Provides a time to nurture your child and show your love.
- Shares your values and beliefs.
- Expresses emotions, such as sadness, happiness, fear, and contentment, and provides an opportunity to talk about these feelings.
- Provides an opportunity to make positive comments to your child.
- Develops a knowledge of and appreciation for other cultures and ethnic customs and values written about in books.
- Connects reading with other enjoyable social experiences like sitting on your lap, cuddling your child, and talking with her/him.
- Provides an opportunity for your child to bond with you and other family members such as brothers and sisters.

- Provides a pleasant family experience in which lifelong habits and attitudes are formed and passed on to the next generation.
- Influences your child to behave in an appropriate manner.

◆ Academic Reasons

Reading to your child . . .

- Expands her/his information and knowledge base.
- Stimulates your child's interest in science, health, social studies and many other subjects incorporated in children's books.
- Enlarges your child's vocabulary.
- Allows your child to practice making predictions (about the outcome of the story).
- Develops your child's listening skills.
- Increases your child's attention span.
- Develops your child's ability to focus on a single topic.
- Stimulates your child's imagination.
- Develops her/his memory.
- Develops "higher order thinking skills," such as by providing the answers to "Why" and "How" questions. ("Higher order thinking skills" are involved when your child uses clues to provide and explain answers more complex than "Yes/No" or "I don't know.")
- Encourages creativity.
- Motivates your child to want to read.
- Provides time when your child can ask questions and have you answer them.
- Provides time when your child can make comments and form opinions about stories.
- Provides time when your child can compare and evaluate characters in stories.

- Provides time when your child can combine knowledge from previous reading with what she/he is presently reading or hearing read.

◆ **Parent/Caregiver Reasons**

Reading to your child . . .

- Reinforces that you are your child's most influential teacher.
- Satisfies the social and academic needs of your child, which in turn satisfies you.
- Helps you meet the varied and individual needs of your child.
- Satisfies your need to fulfill your parental responsibilities of influencing and monitoring your child's development.
- Develops a bond between you and your child.
- Expands your knowledge of children's literature.
- Expands your knowledge of your child's interests.
- Helps you to establish a link for your child between you and her/his teacher (if your child is school age), and home and school, as together they stress for your child the importance of being a good reader.

Summary Box

You are your child's most influential teacher!

What to Do at Home to Prepare Your Child for School

I know that parents/caregivers want their children to learn as much as possible when they go to school. Parents/caregivers can help make that happen!

Parents/caregivers should understand that a school does not expect them to teach their children to read at home, but rather to acquaint their children with print and all the places where one encounters the printed word. This includes all kinds of children's books and magazines, comic strips and pictures, as well as "environmental print" which is present wherever we go and in whatever we do. That includes street signs, printing on vehicles, billboards, buildings, and on packaged foods. The list is endless.

The most important readiness you can provide for school is to develop within your child a love for and enjoyment of books and stories. When your child has a love for books and enjoys every opportunity to listen to someone read and to discuss what has been read, you have, in part, provided a readiness for learning to read.

There are other ways to help to ensure your child's success with reading and learning. Some of these ways are having your child listen to and follow instructions, focus on a task and complete it, cooperate with the teacher and the other students, and behave well so that the classroom is free from interruptions and distractions. All of the above can be taught during the preschool years and when parents/caregivers read to children. A family reading session requires listening and focusing on what is being read, discussing the story by taking turns in talking and asking questions, and behaving in a manner so that all can hear and enjoy the story. A family reading session, or a parent/caregiver reading to one child, provides opportunities to prepare children for learning to read.

When children have not had the advantage of parents/caregivers reading to them, these children's first teacher at school must spend time with the children to prepare them for the teaching of reading by acquainting the students with the printed word and its meaning by using the ideas such as those that follow. These ideas should be considered a parent's responsibility from the time your child is born. When this is not done, it means that some children must spend precious instructional time at the beginning of their school years doing activities that they could have learned in the home before they started school.

There is some speculation that even reading to your child before birth sets the stage for their enjoyment of and attitude toward reading as a young child. Shortly after reading about this, I had an opportunity to test this belief while caring for our newly born grandson, Zachary. At the time, Zachary's older brother, Tyler, was five and his parents had read to Tyler daily. It was interesting to note that when Zachary was fussy or restless, and his mother began to read to his five-year old brother, Zachary became quiet and ceased to fidget and fuss. It did seem that the baby appeared to associate the reading aloud with relaxation, pleasantness, quiet, and peace. This behavior appeared to be learned before birth and continued immediately following his birth. I have read about the advisability of a mother of a first born child reading aloud from a newspaper, a book, or a magazine each day before her child is born. The unborn child may acquaint this read-aloud time with quiet, peace, stillness, and relaxation, and thus develop a positive attitude toward reading aloud. If research were to find this to be true, we could say that a child's preparation for school even begins before birth!

There are many things that you can do at home that prepares your young child for school. It involves everything you do and say during your child's waking hours. Every incident of every day is a learning opportunity. If the premise is true that your child learns more during the first three years of his/her life than at any other time in his/her life, as research suggests, then you do not want to miss any opportunity to teach your child during this period!

But it is good to know that teaching does not require a shelf full of books or a weekly trip to the library. There are so many learning activities, such as talking to your child about and bringing to his/her attention all the appropriate things we as adults do and say. This may include the names of things you see, as well as colors, numbers, letters, and how they all are related. Many of these learning activities do not cost money or require a lot of time or reading materials. They do require your talking with your child and taking the time to listen to his/her questions. By doing these things you can make a difference in your child's readiness for school and for learning to read.

I recall baking a fresh cherry pie for a friend needing help when our son, Royce, was three and one-half years old. He was standing on a footstool helping me to roll out the pie crust after pitting the cherries and preparing them to be put in the crust. As we finished Royce asked, "Where is our pie?"

I answered, "We only had enough cherries for one pie and we needed to help our friend by making this pie for him."

He answered pensively, "Mom, I wish I were your friend."

I listened to my son's remarks in two ways. I heard what my son said and promised him that with the next picking of cherries we would make a pie for our family. The most important message I heard was that my family should come first, or at least in a top priority category. Sometimes we parents forget how our children perceive our actions.

When my children were young I was a stay-at-home mother, but even then I would assume too many volunteer activities and obligations that may have led my children to feel that they did not come first. You must demonstrate to your family that they are top priority and that they come first. When you do not place your family first, your child may tell you in a subtle way how he/she feels about that. That is what our son did.

You must help your child to develop an inquiring mind and a desire to read and learn on his/her own. From the day your child is born (or perhaps before he/she is born), you should be preparing your child for learning in school. The activities that follow are only a few items from an endless list that you can generate daily as you develop and shape your child's learning. By doing some of these things you are preparing your child to be a successful student in school.

What

to Do at Home to Prepare Your Child for School

◆ Help your child to learn and develop his/her **language skills** by doing the following . . .

- Take walks often. Talk about everything you see—the animals, plants, trees, birds, weather, people, etc.

- Visit a pet store in a shopping mall, or go to a museum or zoo. Ask your child to name the animals and talk about them.

- Plant a tomato, pepper, or other vegetable plant and a flower in the spring. Talk about how they grow. Let your child water the plants. Have your child pick the peppers and/or tomatoes when it is time, and prepare and serve them with your family meal.

- Pick a flower and place it in your home. Talk with your child about its colors and beauty.

- If possible, stop and watch a farmer planting crops or harvesting them. Talk about the uses of the crop, particularly if your child can relate to those uses. For example, if corn is being harvested, ask your child: "What do you eat that has corn in it?" The answer could be corn on the cob, corn meal

muffins, popcorn, and corn or frosted flakes. Also talk with your child about the animals on the farm that eat corn.

- Take your child to a park to play. Have your child name the playground equipment, such as the slide, the swing, the merry-go-round, and the jungle gym. Your child can also learn about taking turns, sharing, and playing safely on the equipment.

- Plan a family picnic and talk with your child about the food you are serving. For example, discuss the shape, color, how and where it grows, and its nutritional value.

- Do finger plays with your child.

- Read your child books and talk about the pictures in the books that help to tell the story.

- Tell your child stories about your own childhood, your school experiences, and the games you played.

- Make up stories together. You will start the story. Then your child will add the next sentence or part. You should provide a sentence that is easy for your child to build on each time you add your part to the story.

- Ask your child to tell you his/her favorite story.

- Talk about everything your child does and sees from babyhood on, so that your child will learn about the world he/she lives in. Your child will also learn many words and their proper usage. In this way, your child's language skills will develop, he/she will become interested in many things, and will be eager to learn more about many different topics in school through reading.

- Help your child to memorize nursery rhymes and poems.

- Sing songs with your child.

- Have your child clap, hop, and skip to music.

- Choose a favorite recipe and with your child's help, cook, bake, and serve it to your family or friends. Have your child describe the dish and its ingredients.

- Listen to audio tapes or CDs of singing and story telling as your child follows along in the accompanying book. This may be done at home or in the car while traveling. This helps your child to listen, to follow a story in a book, and to understand a story.

- Talk with your child about what you see as you are driving in the car. Scan signs and billboards for numbers and all the letters of the alphabet, or those in your child's name.

- See how many states you can list by observing the license plates of other cars when you and your child are traveling. Have your child repeat the name of each state listed.

- If your child is school age, talk about school every day. Ask your child at least one question per day about school. Expect an answer that gives you an idea about what happened at school that day. If your child has difficulty answering, gently question him/her until you elicit something about their day. Make positive comments about what your child tells you.

- Give your child jobs to do at home such as picking up toys, making his/her bed, and helping with the dishes. This teaches your child the identification of daily work and jobs, it helps your child to listen to adult requests and to follow directions, and to be responsible for and complete a task. If your child has not done the job satisfactorily, help him/her to do the task according to your expectations by explaining it to him/her and demonstrating how the task is to be done. (When assigning chores, please keep in mind the age of your child and remember that your expectations should be in accordance with your child's level of development and his/her ability to understand the job to be done.) When he/she has done the task, praise your child! Your child will enjoy continuing this work if you appreciate his/her efforts. In this way, your child will learn from you how to praise and make positive comments about fulfilling job responsibilities. This carries over as well to the tasks a teacher will assign at school.

- Make family rules with your child and expect your child to follow them. Post the rules, and have your child repeat them.

◆ Help your child to learn **specific facts about reading** by teaching the following . . .

- The picture on the cover of a book usually tells something about the story.
- A book has a front and back cover.
- Print is read from top to bottom in the United States.
- Print is read from left to right in the United States.
- Print has meaning. It says something.
- Spaces are used to separate words.
- Punctuation also helps to separate words, and to interpret a story.
- Pages are turned one at a time. They are turned from front to back in the United States.
- Books are written by a person called an author.
- The pictures are created by a person called an illustrator.
- A story or book has a beginning, a middle, and an ending.
- Looking at the pictures can help to predict what will happen in a story or book.
- Predicting can add interest and fun to reading. Predictions do not have to be correct.
- There are many forms of literature, such as poetry, fantasy, fiction, and nonfiction.

◆ Provide a time **after reading a story or book** when your child can . . .

- Comment on the story.
- Ask questions about the story.

- Compare and contrast the characters in the book or story.
- Evaluate the characters—who was right or wrong, and why.
- Combine new information with knowledge learned through previous reading.
- Compare the story with other stories about a different era of time, different problems or themes, different cultures, or different areas of world.

Summary Box

You are your child's first teacher!

How to Select Books for Your Child

There are many ways to select books for children! Lists are available on children's favorite books. Teachers may have access to a list that is published each year in the *Reading Teacher*. Librarians have access to a list that is developed by the American Library Association. Other lists appear in books related to the subject of reading. Public libraries and book stores sometimes list children's books that are most often read by children and adults. Some of these lists may even be published in your local newspaper. A best seller's list based on book sales in various parts of the country may be available. These lists are excellent resources, but parents/caregivers should remember that selecting books with their child can be a favorite family activity, and can be done without the help of these lists! The experience of choosing a book is a learning activity in and of itself for your child.

Public libraries offer opportunities for each child who has a library card to select several books. This allows for children and parents/caregivers to be more adventurous in selecting books, and it certainly is better than buying a book your child does not like. Checking numerous books out from the library at no cost allows children to select books that they may not like. This process enables children to sample a variety of books that focus on many different topics. It helps them to determine their interests.

When the opportunity exists for your child to check out more than one book, she/he can develop new interests through exploring books on a variety of subjects. Your child can learn about the various formats of books. Children's books can be large, small, poetic, rhyming, creative, imaginative, pop-up, colorfully illustrated, make believe, true life happenings, a story from the author's life or one written about another person's life, about an animal or even a silly make-believe character.

Unlike many public libraries, school libraries usually have a book limit, so your child cannot be quite as adventurous in selecting books there. If school age, your child will often choose to read books that her/his peers are reading. A classroom teacher, school librarian, or aide may influence, or actually help, your child to select books that she/he can both read independently and would enjoy reading.

If public or school libraries are not available, exposing your child to a wide variety of interests, forms of literature, and kinds of books becomes more difficult. Perhaps a neighborhood exchange of books is possible. Searching for and finding children's books at a reasonable cost at garage sales or flea markets may be fun for your family. Old books may be found in this way, as well as in the attics of grandparents and other relatives. There may be a historical value in reading old books. The illustrations which depict a different era can be very intriguing to some children. The language of that era and the way of life and expectations for the children of another generation may open a new door of learning for your child. Interest in the past can lead to the reading of favorite stories of preceding generations, and can develop an interest in history.

Your child can have many experiences through reading. I often use traveling by reading as an example. "Travel" in the United States and to other lands is possible through a book. A story that takes place in Africa or China provides an opportunity to learn about places and people that your child may never see or visit firsthand. If your child does travel later in life, it will make her/his travels more interesting as she/he verifies the information and the visual images your child had of that far off land from a book or story read many years prior to the visit. Books that reveal how others live and the questions that arise from that knowledge makes reading with your child a great responsibility as she/he begins to under-stand our multicultural world through the printed word and through your shared opinions, values, and beliefs. Your selection of books, then, should include those that have a multicultural focus such as those discussed.

I have always told parents/caregivers that it is good to read to their children! But just reading to them without asking questions or having a discussion about them makes your family reading only half as good as it could be. The questioning and discussion are very important when reading. Books about people and places different from that of your child and family causes your child to ask questions and make comments. Remember that questioning about the story can motivate your child to want to read more. In this way your child may become an independent reader who can learn on her/his own.

There is no right or wrong way to choose books to read. There are some books that you may or may not want your child to read because of your values, your religious beliefs, and/or your personal preferences. All of these criteria are acceptable. In fact, it is good and desirable that you can influence your child and her/his selection of books in this way. Book offerings in a library are usually diverse and large enough to serve many parents/caregivers' and children's preferences and needs.

In the primary grades, children can find books that they can read by finding a book at their independent level of reading, which is generally about one year below their instructional level. You can check with you child's teacher for the instructional level. Another way to find books your child can read independently is by using the "five finger test." This is done by having your child select a page in the book that she/he would like to read. As your child reads aloud, words missed on the page are counted on your fingers. If your child misses five or more words on the page, the book is probably inappropriate and too difficult a reading level for your child.

Remember—be adventurous in your child's book selection. It will open doors to new experiences, interests, and **learning**!

How

to Select Books for Your Child

- Allow your child to choose books herself/himself.

- Assist your child in choosing books.

- Take turns (parents/caregiver and child) choosing books.

- Choose books based on your child's current interest.

- Ask other children around your child's age what their favorite books are.

- Ask the school librarian or library aide for the books that children of your child's age most often check out.

- Ask the public library's librarian or aide for a list or recommendations of young children's favorite books.

- Ask your child's teacher, if your child is school age.

- Ask the salespeople who work in the children's department of local book stores about the best sellers.

◆ Read catalogs that sell children's books. These are usually available from a teacher, or the school or public library.

◆ Read books written about reading which contain book list for children, such as James Trelease's *Read Aloud Handbook* (Penguin, 1995).

◆ Select books your child **can read to you** by . . .

- Choosing books that have a lot of patterns and repetition for beginning readers.
- Choosing books with big print for beginning readers.
- Choosing books in which pictures support the text or what is read.

◆ Select books you **can read to your child** by . . .

- Choosing a book one to three years **above** your child's instructional level. You may need to check with your child's teacher or a librarian for the instructional level.
- Choosing a book that can open a new door to learning or develop a new interest for your child.
- Choosing books based on your child's current interests that you know she/he would like.
- Choosing a variety of types of books to read, such as nonfiction, poetry, myths, and books that may relate to subjects that are commonly taught in school, such as science, health, music, social studies, and others.
- Choosing a variety of books which are at your child's independent reading and instructional level.

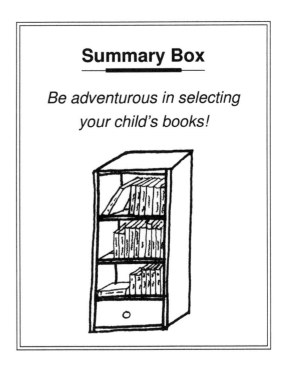

Summary Box

Be adventurous in selecting your child's books!

What to Do When You Do Not Have Books to Read

Sometimes there is a lack of reading materials or books to read in the home because you and your child could not go to the library, your child forgot his/her books at school, or your child does not want to read the books that you have at home. When that occurs there are many activities you can do with your child that are as important and helpful as book and story reading. These activities give you and your child or family an opportunity to be creative and imaginative. They can provide as much enjoyment and learning opportunities as a reading session. There are also ways to vary your family reading sessions.

It is important that you explore these alternative activities so you can demonstrate to your child your willingness and eagerness to be flexible so that he/she can learn, and so that learning occurs in many ways and in a variety of circumstances. Within each individual child and adult is a resourcefulness that enables each of us to be a problem solver and a decision maker, and the alternative activities following provide an opportunity to put these skills to use.

Today we are surrounded by many colorful books, magazines, advertisements, packaged foods, signs, and computer programs that require us to read, think, analyze, and make decisions from among many choices. Many of the suggestions that follow embody these opportunities to learn. But you should also be involved in these choices. Your child needs your help to guide him/her through the mounds of printed materials and to make beneficial choices.

I refer to these sorts of printed materials as "environmental print." They are everywhere. We cannot escape them. Therefore, we need to give our children an opportunity to explore them and use them in a way that will be beneficial and meaningful to them. This practice can prevent them from making poor choices later in their life. When they have had experience in working with environmental print and making choices in a positive way, it will help them to avoid making undesirable choices later. For example, a shoe advertisement may claim that you will be able to run faster, will become a member of the "in" group, or be a pace setter in fashion if your wear their shoes. There are choices to be made everyday with everything we buy. Children who have had discussions with their parents/caregivers on this subject have a better idea of how to "sort out" the important, relevant facts of shopping and make easier choices. This is the kind of opportunity that environmental promises for parents/caregivers and their children. When we use these alternative reading materials and ideas, we are exposing our children to the real world of print and giving them experiences in how to use it beneficially.

It would be helpful if you kept either a basket or box where you can gather and assemble your materials for an environmental print reading session. Materials might include scissors, paper (recycled, if possible), highlighting pens, magic markers, ink pens, pencils, paste or glue, and various sizes of paper bags. The kitchen table, the family room floor, or your child's bedroom can be your work space. I challenge you to make this experience of working with environmental print a fun and enjoyable family time. I know you can do it if both you and your child use your imaginations!

I recall spending a similar session with our children around the kitchen table prior to a spring holiday. I had saved the advertisements, catalogs, and fliers that focused on that holiday. Instead of each child reading a book or story, we worked together on a spring holiday project. Our preschooler, Mylla, made a collage of many colors for a small table cover. She cut out some flowers, glued them to pipe cleaners, placed them in a vase, and put the vase on top of the collage. Our second grader, Royce, planned a holiday breakfast by cutting out appropriate food pictures from grocery store fliers, along with the price per item. He then computed the total cost for the meal. Our fifth grader, Lyndell, chose a holiday outfit for each child and computed the cost per child and the total cost for the family.

What did they learn? They learned that working together and sharing ideas was fun for everyone. They became exposed to a kind of reading that is important to everyday living as adults. They learned that everything they worked with that day had a cost, and that proper planning and budgeting was important so that the family did not spend more than they earned. Those are important lessons! This type of activity can be accomplished by combining your individual children's reading time and allowing some extra time (approximately 40 minutes) to complete their tasks and to share them with their family members.

Other activities just as important to healthy, stable family living involve sharing your family's history, telling experiences from your own childhood, and sharing current family experiences that include the good and not so good times. Telling your child about his/her life in the family is always a favorite story that holds children spellbound! They love it!

What

to Do When You Do Not Have Books to Read

- Use advertisements found in grocery, hardware, discount, toy, and drug store fliers.

- Use the weekly newspaper supplement that is delivered to your mailbox sometimes, even if you do not subscribe to a newspaper.

- Use community newspapers, as well as other free brochures, booklets, etc.

- Use catalogs from mail order houses.

- Use any magazines or periodicals that are available.

- Use cereal boxes and other boxed grocery items with pictures, comics, etc.

- Use billboards, road signs, movie marquees, storefront signs, restaurant menus, etc.

In each of the above alternatives the reading period of ten minutes may be used to . . .

- Expand your child's vocabulary by identifying or naming the pictures or the items.

- Identify colors, shapes, sizes, and spatial directions (right, left, east, west, up, down, etc.).

◆ Categorize lists of items by placing vegetables, fruits, dairy products, clothing, tools, toys, etc. in groups and then listing the items in each group. Or, cut pictures of these items out and have your child paste them on construction paper, a grocery bag, newsprint, or recycled office paper.

◆ With your child, count the items you have grouped or cut out.

◆ Identify letters, sounds, and numbers. For example, find all the letters of the alphabet or all the numbers from 1-20.

◆ Talk about weight, such as pounds (lbs.) and ounces (oz.).

◆ Talk about our money system and the symbols for dollars ($) and cents (¢).

◆ Talk about prices as being more or less than other prices.

◆ Create a nutritional meal poster by having your child choose a vegetable, a fruit, a dairy item, a meat (if appropriate), and a bread product.

◆ Locate foods in the Food Guide Pyramid shown in many grocery advertisements and on the packages of many foods.

◆ Create a story and an illustration on poster paper by having your child cut out selected items from advertisement fliers you receive in the mail.

◆ Have your child label items in ads using "invented" spelling (spelling a word like it sounds) and then reading all the words he/she has written.

◆ Develop your own activities for your child by collecting pictures that reflect your child's interests and abilities for use in making a poster, scrapbook, or mural.

◆ Make up rhyming poems or songs. Ask your child to give you a word. Create a simple rhyme based on that word. Your child can help you by adding additional rhyming words that can be incorporated in the poem or song. Then give your child a word and have him/her create a rhyme with your help.

◆ Together read an easy to prepare recipe and prepare the food to share with your family.

◆ Share a story about your life, your school experiences, and games you played as a child. This can build your child's knowledge of your family history and create an interest in his/her family roots.

◆ Tell your child a story about the day he/she was born. Your child will love it!

◆ Create a story cooperatively with your child about his/her life, and have your child illustrate the story.

◆ Use your imagination! I have had parent/caregiver groups generate as many as 30 topics that a parent and child could talk about based upon one grocery advertising flier.

> ## Summary Box
>
> *Not having a book or story to read can result in an enjoyable family activity in which your child learns about environmental print.*

◆ Read a children's periodical or magazine as an alternative to reading a book. The cost of a year's subscription is generally about the same as buying one book. And it is like receiving a new book every month. In addition, children's magazines have many activities such as mazes, crossword puzzles, jokes, etc. The International Reading Association publishes a book, *Magazines for Children* by Donald R. Stahl, which reviews many children's magazines published in the United States on every topic. Recommendations for the suitable age and grade groups are made for each magazine. You can probably find this reference in your local public library.

Where and When to Read With Your Child

Where and when you read with your child is one of the most important decisions you must make in family reading. There may be several places where you can read with your child in your home. This could be on a comfortable sofa, in your child's bedroom, your bedroom, in a rocking chair, or on a soft rug on the floor. The atmosphere surrounding the place where you read should be as pleasant and quiet as possible. Ideally it should be free from distractions, such as other children playing nearby, the television or stereo playing, and other influences that might divert your child's attention. The place you choose should also have adequate lighting.

I suggest that you and your child select that quiet place to read together and return there each day until your habit of reading together becomes a family habit and an everyday event. When this is done, less time will be spent on deciding where to read and more time on the actual reading. Your child will also soon learn that a peaceful, quiet place adds to the enjoyment and relaxation of reading together.

When should you read to your child? Before your child goes to bed is usually a favorite time because reading together is a relaxing time and is conducive to falling asleep. Before nap time is also a good reading time for preschoolers. When preschoolers are bored, get hurt, or simply feel a need for nurturing or contact with a parent/caregiver, reading offers an opportunity to satisfy that need. When your child is ill, reading will break the monotony of bed rest and help relieve her/his discomfort.

Novel and unusual ways have been devised by working parents for reading with their children. When I was principal of Garden Hills Elementary School in Champaign, Illinois, our school had a family reading club, mentioned previously. Children who could already read were asked to spend all or part of their ten-minute reading period reading to their parents/caregivers. One mother listened to her three school age children read while she prepared dinner, washed the dishes, and sorted and folded the laundry. When the father was home, he would read to the children in the living room after they had read to their mother. Other parents took turns reading to their children before their bedtime. Others read with or to their children on Saturday and Sunday, when they had more time. Children who had homework to do did that on weekday evenings while their parents read to their younger siblings who did not have homework or not as much homework.

Even today there is nothing I like better than to listen to someone read! The available audio tapes, CDs, and "talking books" plus the players in cars and other vehicles allow for hours of reading enjoyment while the family travels on vacation or to visit relatives and friends. It is a wonderful way to share family reading with time for discussion and opinions to be expressed.

Parents/caregivers should occasionally involve all their children in a family reading session. For example, this may be done on a night when the family is returning from one of the children's sporting or scout events, or a church or school activity when lack of time prohibits reading with each child individually. There are advantages to a family reading session. When you read to all the children in the family at the same time, the children can learn from one another's conversations and opinions. Everyone should have an opportunity to share information and/or express an opinion in an orderly manner by taking turns when they speak.

The school environment and the home atmosphere differ for reading to children. Although both are quiet and relaxed, the home atmosphere is and should be more intimate. This is a time when you can nurture your child. Your child may need your physical closeness and contact. If you have a young child, she/he can sit on your lap. If your child is older, physical contact is still important, so she/he can sit close beside you on a sofa or in a big chair. You may want to read together by lying beside one another on a bed, or on a soft rug where eye contact can be made and facial expressions can be easily seen and interpreted. You should be close enough so the book can be readily seen by both of you.

Reading together and talking about the stories and books provides the opportunity to respond to your child according to her/his own needs. It provides the individual attention that she/he loves. I am reminded of my teaching experiences with primary grade students. I could usually identify the children who were read to at home. When I was reading to the class, these children seemed to expect and need physical contact, and would somehow find their way into my lap or would stand or sit as close to me as possible.

I also remember my own reading experiences as a parent of three children, with a four-year age span between each child. Our reading time was in the evening just before their bedtime. First I read to Mylla, our youngest child, in a rocking chair while the middle child, Royce, answered the telephone or the doorbell if necessary. During this period he also chose the book he wanted to read and got ready for bed, while our oldest child, Lyndell, did her homework. After the youngest child was tucked in for the night, I read to the Royce on the sofa in the living room. Lastly, Lyndell chose to read in her bedroom. We sometimes took turns reading a paragraph, a page, or even a chapter to one another. We spent a lot of our time discussing what we read and predicted what would happen in the next chapter. She chose to read many books in a series, such as the *Little House on the Prairie* books by Laura Ingalls Wilder. If we read a short chapter together, I would allow her to read another by herself before it was "lights out" time. The next night she would summarize for me the chapter she had read independently, which was an excellent language arts activity for her. If I did not understand her summary or had questions about the chapter, we would discuss those. Sometimes we would search the chapter together for the answers.

When reading to an older child, a parent/caregiver should remember that the listening and comprehension level of a child usually exceeds her/his own reading level. This means that you can read an older child books that are too difficult for her/him to read alone. These books do extend your child's knowledge and provide enjoyment as well. This also encourages and motivates your child to want to become a better reader so that she/he can read these more advanced books independently. Your older child can also read more than the two of you might have time to read together each time. Just as reading to a preschooler motivates her/him to want to learn to read when the child begins school, reading difficult books motivates your older child to want to become a better reader so she/he can read those books independently.

It is important that each child in the family have a special place, such as a shelf, box, or basket where they can keep the books that belong to them. In addition, you may want a special place for the books that are checked out from a library. This could be another box or shelf. In this way you are not always having to sort through all the books in the house looking for ones that need to be returned to the library.

Where and when to read sets the stage and the atmosphere for a rewarding, satisfying, relaxing, and enjoyable time together. It is the foundation of family reading.

Where *and* When

to Read With Your Child

- Choose a reading place in the home, such as a comfortable chair or sofa, in your child's bedroom, the family room, on the floor, or in a rocking chair.

- Choose a place that is relatively quiet, orderly, and free of interruptions.

- During reading time, the telephone or doorbell should be answered by someone else in the family other than the people who are reading.

- Turn off the television!

- Limit nonemergency interruptions from other family members during reading time.

- Consider reading in public places, such as the doctor's office, in restaurants, parks, motels/hotels, airport waiting areas, on buses and trains, or in the family vehicle.

- Establish a daily time for reading.

> ### Summary Box
>
> *Where and when you read with your child provides the foundation for family reading.*

How to Read With Your Child

There are many appropriate ways of reading with your child. Increasing your child's interest in a book or story before you begin reading is an important activity at any age level. You should begin reading a book by introducing the book to the child. This can be done by looking at the cover and even the back of the book for picture clues. If there are no pictures on the book cover, then the title of the book may lend a clue about its contents. If it does not, then you can always say, "Lets read a few pages to find out what this book might be about." When the theme, main characters, and/or setting are revealed, you might stop the reading momentarily and briefly state these facts, which will provide the introduction to the book. You may also ask your child what he/she thinks the book is about. If both of you agree, respond briefly by saying for example, "I agree—good listening/good thinking," and continue reading.

Another activity is to look at a page at the beginning, middle, and end of the book. From those three pages, ask your child to predict what the story or book may be about and how the story may develop. When your child responds, say, "Let's see if you are right." Then begin reading the book.

It was interesting for me as a teacher to observe students (grades 1-8) using this technique to find out what a book was about when they visited the school library. It was a technique they learned from me when I read aloud to them in the classroom. Were they always accurate in their predictions? Most of the time. But they often read those books with renewed enthusiasm to determine if they were accurate! This is a great way to involve your older child in a book before he/she begins reading the book. There are other ideas you can use to involve your child in a story before reading begins, such as dramatizing an incident from the book. Or if you are familiar with the book, simply read some exciting, dramatic paragraphs (usually found at either the beginning or near the end of the book). This will heighten your child's interest in the book.

It is important to ask questions pertaining to the story or book before you begin to read. For example, there may be words, terms, or concepts that need a short explanation for your child to fully understand or interpret the content. This should be done at all age levels. In 1977, a researcher observed parents reading to their preschool children. He reported[**] that the number of questions asked by the parents and the children was one of the best predictors of success on reading readiness scores. Because of these findings, he suggested that questioning occur before, during, and after family reading, with positive remarks made to the children about their responses.

You will note that there are many suggestions for questioning and for discussion following. But there are many others that are not on this list that will occur as a natural outgrowth of your conversations with your child before, during, and after the reading sessions. This is a positive development as you and your child generate questions based on your child's interest, level of understanding, and interpretations. In this process you are individualizing the questioning based on your child's own level of comprehension and interest. The list of suggestions that follows is one that can be used over a period of time. As a starter, chose one item from each category. The quality and quantity of questioning will increase as your child gets older.

There is a higher and lower order of questions. A lower order question is one that a child can answer by recall. An example of this is, "What is the name of the main character?" An example of the higher order question is, "Did you like the main character? Why or why not?" This higher order question may require your child to evaluate what is right or wrong about a character based on his/her experiences and knowledge.

[**] Flood, J. (1977). Parental styles in reading episodes with young children. *The Reading Teacher, 31,* 864-867.

Be alert to the fact that it may be necessary to limit the number of questions, particularly before reading the story, book, or chapter, as there may be even more questions after the family reading. These questions may be about the content, but may also be "deeper" questions involving values, truth, and judgment. These are good kinds of questions, because you as the parent/caregiver will then have an opportunity to express how you feel. Using the theme or characters in a story to talk about your values is a desirable way to express your standards, morals, beliefs, and ethics to your child. Of more importance is that this discussion and sharing of opinions are occurring in a "nonpreaching" situation, and may be more acceptable to your child in this neutral setting with an incident from a book or story. In this situation, your guidance regarding the incident is offered at an unemotional and uninvolved time, when there is more time for reasoning, reflecting, discussion, and decision making.

Remember, this questioning and discussion activity has many benefits. It enlarges and extends the topics of prediction and problem solving in a neutral setting. An example of this is the discussion of a situation in a story where two friends of a boy are always fighting and arguing. They both want the third boy to support them and agree with their solution to the problem. Being able to discuss with you how to handle the experience described in a book provides your child with ideas about how to handle such an incident if and when he/she is faced with it in real life. If clarification and explanation of a viewpoint is needed, you can offer your viewpoint while reading. Hopefully, your child will share your opinions, reflect on them, and apply them to real life situations.

How

to Read With Your Child

- ◆ Before reading a book . . .

    - Look at the cover and back of the book together.
    - Discuss any pictures on the cover, and help your child predict what the book may be about.
    - Relate the pictures to your child's previous experiences or reading.
    - Discuss the title of the book.
    - Look at a picture on a page at the beginning, middle, and end of the book and together predict what the book may be about.
    - Motivate your child to listen to the story by saying, "Let's see if our predictions are right."

- ◆ While reading a book . . .

    - If your child is reading aloud, do not correct his/her reading unless the meaning of the story is lost.
    - When you are reading aloud, vary the loudness, softness, and pitch of your voice.

- Vary your pacing by reading both fast and slow, as appropriate.

- Express the emotions in the story, such as happiness, sadness, contentment, fear, and others, through the use of your voice, your facial expressions, and your body actions. Dramatize the emotional words so your child will understand them. If someone in the story is happy, be a happy, smiling reader. If a character is angry, be gruff. Speak loudly and fast.

- Allow your child to help you read by "reading" any familiar words or parts of the story.

- If your child asks a question that requires a short answer, answer it briefly. Then continue reading so you do not lose the meaning of the story or your child's attention.

- When your child's facial expressions, statements, sleepiness, or other behavior exhibits boredom with the reading, stop your reading or finish the book by quickly telling the rest of the story.

- Use your finger, a file card, or plain paper to glide under the words as you read them. This helps your child to follow along.

◆ After reading a book . . .

- Compliment your child about his/her listening, answering of questions, for sharing his/her opinions, and for expressing his/her feelings. Give specific examples of these behaviors.

- On completing the book reading, ask your child questions such as: (1) "What did you like/dislike about the story?"; (2) "Why did you like/dislike the story?"; (3) "Who was the character you liked best? Why?"; (4) "Who was right/who was wrong? Why?"; (5) "What could have happened?"; and (6) "What was the problem and how was it solved?"

- Ask questions that require more than a "Yes" or "No" answer. If your child answers "Yes" or "No," then ask your child, "Why do you say that?"

- Ask your child to ask you a question about the story.
- Ask your child how he/she would have liked to have changed the story.
- Ask your child if he/she would like to read more books like this one.
- Ask your child if he/she would like to read another book by this author, or one with the same illustrator.
- Ask your child, "What other books that we have read remind you of this book?"
- Ask your child, "What other questions do you have?"
- Ask your child if there are any parts of the book he/she would like to "act out" together.
- Ask your child, "What parts of the book would you like to read again?"

Summary Box

If you do not discuss what you have read, your family reading is only half as good as it could be.

Positive Comments That Can Be Made to Your Child

Positive comments that you make about your child are what she/he responds to, thrives on, and remembers. You are one of the most important people in your child's life, and what you say influences her/his behavior and how your child sees herself/himself. Each reading session provides an opportunity for you to make specific and general positive statements to your child. They will improve your child's performance in reading, and enhance her/his self-concept, self-esteem, and increase her/his enjoyment of your reading together.

Many children have limited time with their parents/caregivers. When they are together there is much to talk about and to do. However, reading sessions can provide an opportunity for the sharing of positive comments. During reading sessions it is important for you to make reading meaningful by relating the content to your young child's life. This will help your child to better understand herself/himself and her/his reading. Reinforcing your child's appropriate reactions and responses with positive comments will encourage your older child to read more, to read a diverse selection of literature, and will result in the development of new interests and an expanded knowledge base.

Positive comments can be either general or specific. General comments are appropriate with individual children as well as with small and large groups of children. General comments are those that praise, support, and influence your child's behavior and actions. They are statements that say to your child, "You are giving good responses, you are meeting my expectations, and I like what you are doing." They inform your child that you approve of her/his performance and want it to continue.

Positive comments also can and should be more specific so that your child can identify her/his own actions and responses that you approve of. These comments can relate more directly to the process of reading and be a statement such as, "I like the way you sounded out that word," or "You did a good job using the other words in the sentence to help you figure out that word."

Specific statements can also relate to your child's preparation for a reading session. You may say, for example, "I like the way you picked up your toys, got ready for bed, chose your book to read, and was waiting for me to read! Good job! We will read a few more pages tonight because you did such a good job! I expect you will do that tomorrow night too."

Each reading session should contain a general and a specific positive comment. The general comment can structure the environment, atmosphere, or climate of the reading session. The specific comment can focus on the process of reading and give your child concrete ideas and examples of how she/he can improve her/his reading behavior or performance. With your encouragement, hopefully your child will want to repeat that behavior or action again and again so that it becomes an integral part of her/his life.

Positive comments made during a reading session can motivate and encourage your child to want to learn to read or to become a better reader. Improved reading will later help your child to learn on her/his own. Anything you can do in your reading sessions or in your family to encourage reading and learning independently will be helpful to your child and to her/his current or future teacher. Every teacher and school desires that kind of parental help and support!

Positive Comments

That Can Be Made to Your Child

While Choosing a Book and Before Reading the Story

◆ General comments can include . . .

- "It will be fun reading this book."
- "I think I will like this book too!"
- "This is a good choice of books!"
- "Let's see if the book is about what you thought it might be."
- "I like your idea, good thought!"
- "Be thinking about who you like in the story or what you like about it. We will talk about that after we have read the book."

◆ Specific comments can include . . .

- "I like the way you are sitting quietly and are ready to read."
- "I like the way you got ready for reading by getting ready for bed and putting your toys away."

- "I like the way you have chosen your books this week. Last night we had a funny story. Tonight it is a book from the alphabet series. I wonder what kind you will choose for tomorrow?"
- "The way you took your bath, brushed your teeth, put on your pajamas, and had your book ready to read was really good tonight. Could you do that again tomorrow night?"

While Reading the Book, or When Your Child Either Pretends to Read or Reads Independently

◆ General comments can include . . .

- "Good reading."
- "Super!"
- "You read that story with lots of expression."
- "Fantastic!"
- "Awesome!"
- "Congratulations."
- "You must be practicing at school. That was good reading."
- "Be proud of yourself—you're a good reader!"
- "Superb."
- "Good listening!"
- "You answered all the questions correctly."
- "You are really paying attention to every word I read."
- "You know a lot of things about the main character."

◆ Specific comments can include . . .

- "I like the way you raised and lowered your voice to act out the story."
- "I like the way you reread that sentence until it made sense to you."
- "I like the way you used the other words in the sentence to figure out the word you did not know."

- "I like the way you paused after that period."
- "I like the way you followed along as I read the story."
- "I like the way you remembered all the details in the story."
- "I like the way you described the setting."
- "I like the way you solved some mysteries in this story before the author told us what happened. Good listening and good thinking!"

After Reading a Book and During the Discussion

◆ General comments can include . . .

- "I think you learned a lot! What do you think?"
- "You were a superb listener."
- "You gave good answers!"
- "What shall we read tomorrow? Be thinking about that!

◆ Specific comments can include . . .

- "Your summary of the story is very good. You can tell me what happened in the beginning, the middle, and the end of the story."
- "You know everything there is to know about the main character—what she/he looked like, how she/he talked, and what she/he was wearing."
- "I like the way you used the picture to figure out the word (say the word)."
- "I like the way you used letter sounds to figure out the word (say the word)."
- "Good thinking when you reread that paragraph so you would understand it."
- Who was your favorite person in this story? Why?" (If your child's answer is, for example, "Because she/he was a good person," you can say, "What did she/he do or say that made her/him a good person?" Your child should be

as specific in her/his answers as you are in your questions.)

- "Your prediction that the bears would come home before Goldilocks woke up was right! How would the story have ended if she awoke and went home before the bears arrived?"

- "Which of those endings do you like the best? Why?"

You will think of many more general and specific positive comments not listed here. Your comments will arise from the story you are reading with your child. They will be as numerous and varied as the books you and your child choose to read together. Each book will generate a new set of positive comments and discussion questions.

Summary Box

Your positive comments increase your child's reading enjoyment, and encourages and motivates her/him to read.

How to Make the Reading/Writing Connection

Making the reading/writing connection could be one of the most helpful, but often overlooked, things parents/caregivers can do to help their children learn to read and write. Many researchers believe that some children learn to read by writing, and others believe that children learn to write by reading. Current teaching methods, strategies, and theories are based on both beliefs as well as a combination of the two.

This knowledge underscores the fact that you need to be certain that your child sees you writing often, and then reading what you have written so your child understands that the two are connected and related. Examples of this are writing a shopping list, checking it by reading it aloud, and then reading it again as you do your shopping. Your child could read the list as you shop and then cross out each item as it is put in the shopping cart. Children almost always request items in a store. But if those things are written on the list at home and then crossed off the list at the store, two things are accomplished during your shopping trip: you are contributing to your child making the reading/writing connection, and you are limiting your child's wish list to the one or two items written on the list.

Children also need to see their parents writing after having read something. An example of this is writing a letter to your child's grandparents in response to a letter you have received from them. In this way your child will see that we write so a message can be read. And when we read a message we sometimes need to write a response.

Sometimes your child sounds out words when reading to determine what the word is. When she/he is writing or reading a word, he/she will use the same sounding out process to spell the word. You may reinforce this process by sounding out words as you read and write with your child. This will help your child see that reading and writing are based on similar phonetic principles. In this way, a connection between reading and writing may be made.

But not all words can be sounded out. These words need to be memorized, and are often referred to as "sight words." Your child's teacher can provide you with a list of these words. Sometimes these words are listed on the back of your child's spelling or reading books. These words can be put on flash cards. You can then show the cards to your child by flashing each card before him/her. Your child should say the word on each card.

You can make a game of identifying "sight words" and words that can be sounded out by having your child collect those cards he/she answers correctly. You keep the cards that he/she answered incorrectly. When you have finished the flash cards, you should each count the number of cards you have. You should praise your child for his/her efforts and for correctly identifying any words on the cards. If he/she has more cards than you, praise your child and read an additional book during your reading session as a reward! The cards you have collected (which are the incorrect words) can be practiced until your child knows these words as well.

Another activity that is helpful to your child while learning sight words is to ask him/her to spell the words aloud while looking at the cards. This helps your child to recognize the letters in the words and later to recall them as he/she writes or reads them. Again your child sees that for every letter in a word there is a written symbol. But in sight words not every letter in the word is "sounded out," and therefore these words have to be memorized. For example, the words "the" and "are" are sight words. You could also write or print a sentence using each sight word on a flash card and ask your child to identify the word in the sentence.

You can also make the reading/writing connection by asking your child to write or print the flash card words. Depending on your child's age, this is a challenging activity! Your child should be rewarded with positive comments for correct responses. When your child uses "invented" spelling (phonetically spells the word) he/she should also be praised for his/her efforts.

There are many activities that you and your child can enjoy while making the reading/writing connection. As you become accustomed to making this a part of your daily reading routine, you will become proficient in developing the reading/writing connection for your child.

A pleasant family reading and writing activity that I enjoyed with our children was to place a note on their pillow before bedtime. It would say, for example, "Have pleasant dreams," "We are having pancakes and sausage for breakfast," or "I have a surprise for you tomorrow." Or I would sometimes place notes on their pillows or bulletin boards in the morning. There were always positive notes. Our children were always anxious to know what the notes said. Before they could read the notes they would say, "Read the note to me," or "What does it say?" I encouraged them to do so on their own in their learning to read days. I would give them clues and hints until they were successful in reading their notes.

How

to Make the Reading/Writing Connection

- Demonstrate to your child that anything that is said, heard, or read can be written.

- With your child, make lists of things you have seen on a trip or walk. Create a story about these items and write it down. Ask your child to illustrate the story. Then read the story together.

- Develop a grocery shopping list, writing it with your child's help.

- Write a rhyming poem or song that the two of you created. Illustrate it, then read it together.

- Make a calendar with your child. For each month, create an illustration and a story or explanation of the picture. Write this on the calendar. Read the story or explanation to your child each month.

- Create a family story. Write about one person, who can be your child, or one of your family members. Read what you wrote to your child.

- With your child, write letters to grandparents, aunts, uncles, cousins, and family friends. Read them before sending them, and read their responses when received.

(age 11)

(age 6)

◆ Label pictures in all kinds of advertisements and read them with your child.

◆ Ask your child to create a picture with colored pencils, finger paints, crayons, or magic markers. (You may use recycled computer printout and copy machine paper, as well as all sizes of paper bags rather than drawing paper.) Have your child label what he/she has created.

Then write on the back or the bottom of the picture a word, sentence, or paragraph of a story based on your child's picture. Read this together.

◆ Encourage your young child to write/scribble (depending on his/her age) on a piece of paper. Ask your child to verbally share what he/she has written.

◆ Encourage your young child to write about a topic of his/her choice. Ask your child to share with you what he/she has written. "Invented" spelling (words spelled phonetically) may be used by your child.

◆ Encourage your child to write about his/her experiences. This will be an easy task because it is something that happened to him/her.

◆ Use pictures for "story starters." Discuss a picture with your child. Then have your child create a story about the picture. If your child cannot yet write, you will need to write the story as your child creates it. Read the story together.

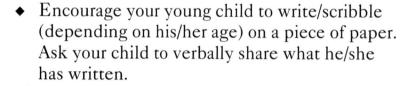

Summary Box
You can demonstrate the reading/writing connection by writing a note to your child every day and reading it to him/her.

Summary

In this section I have shared with you what you can do when you read with your child. I often say to the audiences of my presentations, "If you learned one thing today that you will use tomorrow, then my trip will have been worthwhile." I feel the same way about this guide. If there is one item that you have read that will make your family reading a more enjoyable experience, or enlarge your child's knowledge, that will be the best compensation I could receive.

Parents, caregivers, and teachers determined what the content of this guide should be. They also suggested how it should be presented so that it was easy to follow and read. You can be confident that what you have read is what other parents said they wanted to know. It is also what teachers said their students should know before the formal teaching of reading begins.

The big pay-off for reading to children came when I became a grandparent of two grandchildren. They say to me, "My Dad said we should read that book about Daniel Boone," and "Aunt Lyndell said, 'Have grandma read those books about Abraham Lincoln,'" and "Aunt Mylla said, 'We should read the old Dr. Seuss books.'" History repeats itself when it is bedtime! Just as our children did, my grandchildren too want just one more story and one more book to be read before they are tucked in. But isn't it wonderful that these two grandsons, Tyler and Zachary, love to read the books our family read together? It gives them pleasure to read the "old books" and it brings back the pleasant memories of our family reading sessions and all the things we learned and thought about.

On our summer vacations my three children could spend their savings and allowances for a remembrance, but one item I specified they had to buy was a book about the place we had visited. I can tell you that most of the mementos they purchased have disappeared, but the books remain. They read them today at ages 38-45 to recall the places we visited.

Books sometimes are what connect one generation to the next generation. That happened in our family because I kept the books our children loved. I hope it happens in yours! Our children are not at our house anymore, but the books and their memories are! On Lyndell's last visit she asked about the book classics she had collected some 35 years ago. They are in the attic now. But I must bring them down! She or I would have a great time reading those books to Tyler and Zachary.

Last winter I bought the first full-length, unabridged book that I read as a fifth grader some 60 years ago, *A Girl of the Limberlost* by Gene Stratton Porter. She wrote the book in the early 20th century. The new edition is being published by Gramercy Books and distributed by Random House Value Publishing. Its concern for the vanishing swampland of northeast Indiana in 1900-1920 is similar to the environmental concerns we have today. I cannot wait to read it to Tyler and Zachary who are so concerned about the vanishing species of birds, butterflies, and insects. They will be interested to know that children were concerned about that 100 years ago.

Books give our children knowledge, joy, laughter, and enjoyment. If they have books to read of their mother and father's generation and their grandparents' generations it provides in part the stability, the security, the interests, and the concerns that connect one generation to the next and give our children a sense of belonging and purpose. But most of all, it tells them that the generations before them valued reading and cared enough to save their favorite books for them to read.

Section Three

Appendices

Appendix I:
A Brief Review of Reading Research

Appendix II:
Family Reading Club Information

Appendix III:
Reading Partners Program

Appendix I: A Brief Review of Reading Research

As long ago as 1908, E.B. Huey, in *The Psychology and Pedagogy of Reading*, made the statement: "The secret of it all lies in the parents' reading aloud to and with the child" (p. 332). This statement could easily be said to reflect today's thinking about the value of parents/caregivers' reading aloud to their children. Many educators and researchers feel that there is a positive relationships between being read to at home and various aspects of oral and written language development in children at school (Chomsky, 1972; Durkin, 1966; Harkness, 1981). Almost every reading methods textbook and early childhood education textbook, plus numerous articles, recommend that parents/caregivers read to their young children in order to prepare them well for the learning that will take place in school. Supporting these beliefs in the past century are studies that have shown that reading to children can be a very important facet of becoming literate and developing a positive attitude toward reading that will be carried throughout life.

A Shift in Research Theories

Theories about reading have gradually shifted during the past 20 years from a focus on analysis of the reading process and its various component skills to the examination of reading in its total language context. The two approaches are fundamentally different.

The difference between the philosophies of the "skills" group and the psycho-linguists, or the "whole language" group, is really a difference in perceiving how one learns. Both groups would agree on the goals of reading instruction, but they would differ on how to achieve those goals. The "skills" group suggest that in order to understand the whole process of reading one must first master the smaller aspects, or the component skills of reading, such as visual perception, auditory memory, and knowledge of and application of phonics rules (Samuels, 1976). The other group believe that literacy development is a continuation of the natural language learning for all children. Natural language is based on the assumption that children are immersed in language from the beginning, and from the whole they learn to differentiate the parts, understand general language rules, and create their own expression.

The psycholinguists have come to regard reading as a "whole process" which is learned in the same way that one learns speech. It is another form of communication between writer and reader. Like speech, they believe that reading is learned by immersion in language from which one gradually learns to discriminate the component parts and form the abstract rules that one can apply to new situations (Harkness, 1981).

If we assume that reading is a form of communication that is acquired in the same way that oral language is, then we must investigate all the things that are necessary prerequisites for learning to read. A job of both educators and parents/ caregivers, then, would be to determine the best way to provide these prerequisites to young children.

▬ Prerequisites to Reading

Harkness (1981) has provided us with a list of prerequisites for learning to read based on the view of reading as a whole process and learned in the same fashion as oral language:

1. The child must first of all be immersed in print in order to "hear" complete units of written language so that he will become accustomed to it and be able to form his own rules about the structure of the language. It has been observed, for example, that children who are good readers are often very good at phonics, and the inference is made that a knowledge of phonics makes a good reader. The reverse may be just as true, however; the child who has had a great deal of

exposure to print and has become a good reader may have learned phonics coincidentally.

2. Children must be motivated to respond to print. Babies are motivated to talk to gain approval and manipulate their surroundings. The need for reading is less obvious. If reading is going to require active participation as well as some physical effort, the effort must have some reward in the form of enjoyment or usefulness.

3. Children must have the knowledge that print is meaningful. Children learn through development and practice what sounds are appropriate for delivering oral messages. In the same way they learn that marks on paper can convey meaning.

4. Children must have enough vocabulary and at least an adequate background of knowledge to be able to understand what is printed.

5. Children must be prepared in some way to face the differences between written and oral language.

6. Children must be able to inhibit what seems to be the natural tendency to leap forward in the text when unable to give the necessary attention to a passage long enough to understand it.

▬ Providing the Prerequisites by Reading Aloud

If a job of both parents/caregivers and educators is to determine how best to provide these prerequisites to reading instruction, it would seem that the necessary step to take would be to assure that each child is immersed in written language by being read to at as early an age as possible. Goodman and Goodman (1979) have referred to this as the "lap method" of teaching reading. It is something that conscientious parents/caregivers have been doing for years.

One of the earliest studies of young readers was done by Durkin (1966). Her findings are relevant:

> *First, in doing the research itself, it became clear that early readers are not a special brand of children who can be readily identified and sorted by tests. Rather, it would seem, it is their mothers who play the key role in effecting the early achievement. The homes they provide, the example they show, the time they give to the children, their concepts of their role as educator of the preschool child—all of these dimensions of home life and of parent-child relationships appeared to be of similar importance to the early reading achievement described in this report* (p. 138).

Durkin's findings have major implications to parents/caregivers: The children who learn to read early are the ones who have been read to!

In another early study of successful young readers, Clark (1976) observed that a characteristic common to them all was a home environment that was centered around varied experiences and numerous books and magazines. She pointed out that of most importance seemed to be the presence of an interested adult with time to spare to interact in a stimulating, encouraging way. Clark's young subjects displayed above average abilities in auditory memory and sequencing. Being read to and having reading materials in the home have definite positive effects on children's learning. And this proficiency with complex grammatical forms is enhanced with regular oral reading by parents/caregivers at the preschool level (Durkin, 1978; McCormick, 1983).

The research shows that many aspects of reading knowledge are enhanced by reading aloud to children. These skills include the ability to differentiate between the front and back of a book, awareness of the direction in which print is to be read, and understanding that print provides salient information. The development of these skills is associated with regular story reading at the preschool level (Durkin, 1974; Teale, 1978).

Freeman and Wasserman (1987) found that motivation to deal with the process of learning to read is fostered in children who are read to consistently at home. Children of school age, beginning formal instruction of reading, can also benefit from consistent story reading. Feitelson, Kita, and Goldstein (1986) reported that the comprehension skills and decoding ability of low socioeconomic first grade children read to daily for six months were superior to their control group.

▬ Reading Aloud in Early Childhood—Parents/ Caregivers' Responsibility

Supported by this research which suggests that children's language and literacy development is interwoven and continuous from infancy onward, it is now known that language, literacy, and a love of literature are largely learned at home. As Dorothy Strickland says, "It is very exciting that researchers in various disciplines have recently confirmed the integrated 'birth on' approach long intuitively known . . . " (cited in Strickland & Morrow, 1989).

Learning to read is a continuous process which begins in infancy with exposure to oral language, written language, books, and stories. The role of the parent/ caregiver is key to a child's successful learning. Both Piaget's (Piaget & Inhelder, 1969) and Vygotsky's (1978) theories support this assumption. Piaget believed that children acquire language in association with their activities. He felt that not only language but all activities that involve thought are learned as the result of activity and interactions. Vygotsky believed also that children learn from their interactions with adults. He was convinced that children learn language only with the assistance of an adult. This learned oral language, then, is the basis for learning to read.

In light of the importance of early language and literacy development, the role of the parents/caregivers cannot be understated. There is nothing that can take the place of good role models and exposure to language and literacy in children's early years. When parents/caregivers read to their children at home, their children's later language and reading achievement are positively influenced (Chomsky, 1972; Mason, Peterman, & Kerr, 1989).

New Research Directions

Regardless, as Toomey (1986) emphatically states, "We need no more studies telling us that involving parents in home reading is a useful strategy. That has already been confirmed." What we do need is specific information about the most beneficial ways for parents/caregivers to provide this early reading to every child—such as the ideas and strategies contained in this book.

There is a genuine need for parents/caregivers to be acquainted with reading techniques, strategies, and home-centered activities. As Burket (1981) points out:

> *. . . in order for parents to help their children in the area of reading, they must be guided or directed in appropriate activities. And in order for the teachers to best guide and inform the parents, the teachers must be guided and informed of ways that will work best in accomplishing this. Many of these activities are already being performed naturally by some parents. However, being aware of their value and their availability would be a tremendous aid to all parents and ultimately, all children . . . .*

The primary purpose of parents/caregivers reading aloud to their children is for pleasure. But a number of different activities may be used to increase the benefits as well as the enjoyment of story reading. The research offers specific suggestions for quality reading:

1. **The Nature of the Questions**: Cochran-Smith (1984) noticed that the quantity and the nature of the questions and comments by both parents/ caregivers and the children determine how effective story reading is in promoting readiness for reading.

2. **Shared Reading**: Children who are not yet able to read should be encouraged to join in or read in place of the parent/caregiver whenever possible (Holdaway, 1982). Predictable books, or those with recurring phrases or sentences, are the most appropriate for this

activity. This can be done easily by stopping and waiting for the child to say the refrain while the parent/caregiver sweeps her/his hand under the text to identify the printed form of the child's spoken words. Another form of this activity is to have the child read along with the parent/caregiver or with a taped recording of the story, trying to match the words she/he sees with the words she/he hears.

3. **Repeated Readings**: Research also supports multiple readings of the same story. This has been found to encourage increasing amounts of discussion with each reading (Martinez, 1983; Yaden, 1988). Children should listen to the same story as often as their interest allows. Each reading allows the child to direct his/her attention to different aspects of the story (Martinez & Rosa, 1985).

4. **Children as Story Tellers**: Having the child become the storyteller is a strategy directed at making storytime an intensely personal experience for the child. An important benefit of this strategy is the development of a sense of a story and awareness of story elements such as the beginning, time, location, characters, and ending (Hough, Nurss, & Wood, 1987).

5. **Oral Retelling of Stories**: A beneficial activity is having the child retell the story orally after the story has been read aloud (Golden, 1984; Morrow, 1985). Young children may need assistance, and prompts can be helpful. For example: "Who was the story about?" or "What was the problem the main character had to face?" Consistent instructions with story retelling has been found to improve comprehension (Brown, 1975; Gambrell, Pfeiffer, & Wilson, 1985) and oral language (Morrow, 1985).

6. **Acting Out a Story**: Encouraging children to develop a play from a story is recommended as an activity for creating interest in reading (Cox, 1988; Stoodt, 1988). Grey's 1987 study suggests that acting our stories increases children's comprehension.

7. **Time Spent on Reading Aloud**: The amount of time spent reading aloud to children is a significant factor in fostering literacy acquisition. Shanahan and Hogan (1983) report that the most significant factor in predicting children's achievement on a test of print awareness is the minutes per week spent on book reading.

8. **Reflection**: The quality of the time spent reading is of utmost importance. The child must be allowed some opportunity to reflect upon the stories that were read. One way a parent/caregiver can help to encourage this is to ask the child to relate the things that happened in the story to her/his own situation. For example: "What was the story trying to say? Have the same things ever happened to you?" Miles (1985) refers to these activities as "making meaning with a story."

9. **Individual Reading Time**: Having an opportunity to quietly read a book by herself/himself or to share a story with friends is also important (Kaisen, 1987). Even children who cannot yet read should have time to be alone with their books, to personally reflect on them and to "rehearse" the reading process (Holdaway, 1979).

10. **Quality Books**: The quality of the books chosen to be read aloud to children is an important factor. Anecdotal accounts and research reports both suggest that stories with certain features are suitable for creating a beneficial read-aloud experience. These features include repetitive, rhythmic refrains (Chandler & Baghban, 1986); colorful or imaginative pictures (Martin, 1978); and easily identifiable plots and sequences of events (Stein, 1979).

▬ The Home/School Connection

Research has shown us how important it is that parents/caregivers take a positive and active role in the development and reinforcement of their children's reading skills. Both educators and parents/caregivers must try to develop supportive partnerships to do what is best for children. Past reading research has focused on how to bring this about. Researchers have examined the schools' role and the teachers' role in bringing early reading experiences to all children. Rutherford and Edgar (1970), in their work on parental involvement in children's learning, point out there are two prerequisites to parental involvement: trust between education professionals and parents/caregivers, and a belief by the education professionals that parents/caregivers should be involved in childhood programs. They feel that the latter cannot be compromised: "Parents believe they are a crucial component of education; the government believes it; and research supports it. Unless teachers share this belief, however, there can be no effective teacher-parent cooperation."

Since the research of Rutherford and Edgar, a shift has occurred in how educators view parental involvement in the schooling of their children. In 1992, I conducted a study: "Teachers' Views of Chapter [now know as Title] 1 Programs." This was an item survey with questions on parental involvement. The one question that received the most unanimity from the 913 respondents was the question that asked "To what extent do parents and home life affect a child's learning in school?" The results follow:

Options	% Respondents
One of the important influences	52
Profoundly important	45
Somewhat important	2
Overemphasized influence	.2
Other	.4

I believe that the time was never better than it is now for home and school to cooperate and collaborate so that parents and teachers can maximize the learning for all children. After reading this guide, please be a part of the growing number of parents who actively participate in their children's learning by reading with them.

▬ References

Barbour, J.A. (1995). The outcomes of a teacher training workshop on parent education focusing on reading with children (Doctoral dissertation, University of Illinois).

Brown, A. (1975). Recognition, reconstruction, and recall of narrative sequences of preoperational children. *Child Development*, *46*, 155-166.

Burket, L.I. (1981). *Positive parental involvement in the area of reading during preschool years and primary grades*. (ERIC Document Reproduction Service No. ED 216 324)

Chandler, J. & Baghban, M. (1986). Predictable books guarantee success. *Reading Horizons*, *26*, 176-178.

Chomsky, C. (1972). Stages in language development and reading exposure. *Harvard Educational Review*, *42*, 1-33.

Clark, M.M. (1976). *Young fluent readers*. London: Heinemann Educational Books.

Cochran-Smith, M. (1984). *The making of a reader*. Norwood, NJ: Ablex.

Cox, C. (1988). *Teaching language arts*. Boston: Allyn & Bacon.

Durkin, D. (1966). *Children who read early*. New York: Teachers College Press.

Durkin, D. (1974). A six-year study of children who learned to read in school at the age of four. *Reading Research Quarterly*, *10*, 9-61.

Durkin, D. (1978). *Teaching young children to read* (2nd ed.). Boston: Allyn and Bacon.

Feitelson, D., Kita, B., & Goldstein, Z. (1986). Effects of listening to stories on first graders' comprehension and use of language. *Research in the Teaching of English*, *20*, 339-356.

Freeman, E.B. & Wasserman, V. (1987). A will before there's a way: Preschoolers and books. *Reading Horizons*, *27*, 112-122.

Gambrell, L., Pfeiffer, W., & Wilson, R. (1985). The effects of retelling upon reading comprehension and recall of text information. *Journal of Educational Research*, 216-220.

Golden, J. (1984). Children's concept of story in reading and writing. *The Reading Teacher*, *37*, 578-584.

Goodman, K. & Goodman, Y. (1979). Learning to read is natural. In L. Resnick & P. Weaver (Eds.), *Theory and practice in early reading* (Vol. 1). Hillsdale, NJ: Erlbaum.

Grey, M.A. (1987). A frill that works: Creative dramatics in the basal reading lesson. *Reading Horizons*, *28*, 5-11.

Harkness, F. (1981). Reading to children as a reading readiness activity. *Viewpoints in Teaching and Learning*, *57*, 39-48.

Holdaway, D. (1979). *The foundation of literacy*. Sydney: Ashton Scholastic.

Holdaway, D. (1982). Shared book experience: Using favorite books. *Theory into Practice*, 293-300.

Hough, R.A., Nurss, J.R., & Wood, D. (1987). Tell me a story. *Young Children*, *43*, 6-12.

Huey, E.B. (1908). *The psychology and pedagogy of reading*. New York: Macmillan.

Kaisen, J. (1987). SSR/Booktime: K and 1st grade. *The Reading Teacher*, *40*, 532-537.

Martin, B. (1978). The making of a reader. In Cullinan (Ed.), *Children's literature in the reading program*. Newark, NJ: International Reading Association.

Martinez, M. (1983). Exploring young children's comprehension through story time talk. *Language Arts*, *60*, 202-209.

Martinez, M. & Rosa, N. (1985). Read it again: The value of repeated readings during storytime. *The Reading Teacher*, *30*(8), 782-786.

Mason, J.M., Peterman, C.L., & Kerr, B.M. (1989). *Fostering comprehension by reading books to kindergarten children* (Tech. Rep.). Urbana-Champaign: University of Illinois, Center for the Study of Reading.

McCormick, S. (1983). Reading aloud to preschoolers age 3-6: A review of the research. *Reading Horizons*, *24*, 7-11.

Morrow, L.M. (1985). Retelling stories: A strategy. *Elementary School Journal*, *885*, 647-661.

Piaget, J. & Inhelder, B. (1969). *The psychology of the child*. New York: Basic Books.

Rutherford, R.B. & Edgar, E. (1979). *Teachers and parents*. Boston: Allyn and Bacon.

Samuels, J. (1976). Hierarchical subskills in the reading acquisition process. In J.T. Guthrie (Ed.), *Aspects of reading acquisition*. Baltimore: John Hopkins University Press.

Shanahan, T. & Hogan, V. (1983). Parent reading style and children's print awareness. In J. Niles (Ed.), *Searches for meaning in reading. Thirty-second yearbook of the National Reading Conference* (p. 212).

Stein, N.L. (1979). *The concept of story: A developmental psycholinguistic analysis*. Paper presented at the American Educational Research Association annual meeting, San Francisco.

Stoodt, B.A. (1988). *Teaching language arts*. New York: Harper & Row.

Strickland, D.S. & Morrow, L.M. (Eds.). (1989). *Emerging literacy: Young children learn to read and write.* Newark, NJ: International Reading Association.

Teale, W.H. (1978). Positive environments for learning to read: What studies of early readers tell us. *Language Arts, 55,* 922-932.

Toomey, D.M. (1986). *How parental participation and involvement in schools can increase educational inequality.* Melbourne: A.A.R.E. Conference paper.

Vygotsky, L.S. (1978). *Mind in society: The development of psychological processes.* Cambridge, MA: Harvard University Press.

Wilken, P.A. (1992). *Teachers' views of Chapter 1 programs* (Tech. Rep.). Urbana-Champaign: University of Illinois, Center for the Study of Reading.

Yaden, D. (1988). Understanding stories through repeated read-alouds: How many does it take? *The Reading Teacher, 41,* 556-560.

Appendix II: Family Reading Club Information

Garden Hills Family Reading Club began after I became principal of Garden Hills Elementary School in Champaign, Illinois. It was an idea that a third grade teacher brought to a school advisory committee meeting. She had talked with a teacher from Wisconsin who had established a similar program there. Our group talked about it, and then presented this idea to the entire staff. They agreed that it was needed in our school but only if it were easy to organize and manage.

Our goal was to involve the parents and make them our partners in teaching our students to become independent, better readers. We explained to the parents and the students that it was impossible for one teacher to provide the practice time that was needed for our students to improve their reading. (Probably this is the same situation for **your** child's teacher!) We asked the parents to help us. They did! They read 3,300 hours the first year and 6,000 hours the second year and maintained that amount of family reading for all the years I was principal.

These parents were proud of their participation in their children's learning. They were especially pleased (as were their children) to see the large wooden trees that some of the fathers had constructed and painted filling up with leaves that the children earned by reading. Our custodian climbed a ladder two times every lunch hour to tack the leaves to the tree for the primary and then the intermediate students. It was to the parents' and our student's credit that we continuously and consistently maintained our reading test scores.

Having the "reading trees" in the community room with all their colorful leaves was a reminder to every parent who came to a PTA meeting, a play, or another performance of the good works they were doing. The visual image that the trees provided for the students and the parents motivated them to read more. The second year we had to put up another tree.

If your child's school does not have a reading incentive program, you the parents can be responsible for starting one (with the assistance of the school staff)! Following is information that will tell you how it is done. Good luck and enjoy reading with your children!

Family Reading Club

Dear Parents,

It's new! It's a Family Reading Club!

The staff at _____ has taught your children to become better readers. Their reading achievement has improved this year. Yet we believe our students can become even better readers if we involve all the parents in the reading process.

The Family Reading Club goal is to have your child become an active and enthusiastic reader at home. With your help, your child will learn to appreciate and enjoy the fun of reading. Your child will learn that you believe reading is important. We are looking forward to working with you on this worthwhile project.

Sincerely,

What to Do

◆ Each day we ask that you and your child sit down and read **orally** together for ten minutes. These minutes will count toward your child being awarded a Family Reading Club Certificate.

◆ Children in grades 3, 4, and 5 should read orally to you. Children in grades K, 1, and 2 may be read to by you. We encourage you to have your child read to you as soon as she/he is able. Your child needs to practice reading with you. By practicing, children become better readers.

◆ Each day that you read together for ten minutes, sign the record form.

◆ When you have read orally with your child for a total of 250 minutes, return the record form to your child's teacher. A Family Reading Club Certificate for your child will be placed on the bulletin board in your child's classroom. A leaf, with your child's name on it, will also be placed on the "reading tree."

◆ For each additional 250 minutes of oral reading, a gold sticker will be placed on your child's Family Reading Club Certificate in the classroom.

◆ Every child at _____ is eligible to earn a Family Reading Club Certificate. These certificates will also be awarded to the children publicly at the school awards assembly at the end of the year.

◆ Enjoy your family reading! It should be a pleasant, enjoyable time together! It will help your child become a better reader!

Family Reading Club Record

For the Family of _____ Grade _____

Date	Minutes	Parent/Caregiver Signature	Title of Article or Book, or Other Reading/Language Arts Activity

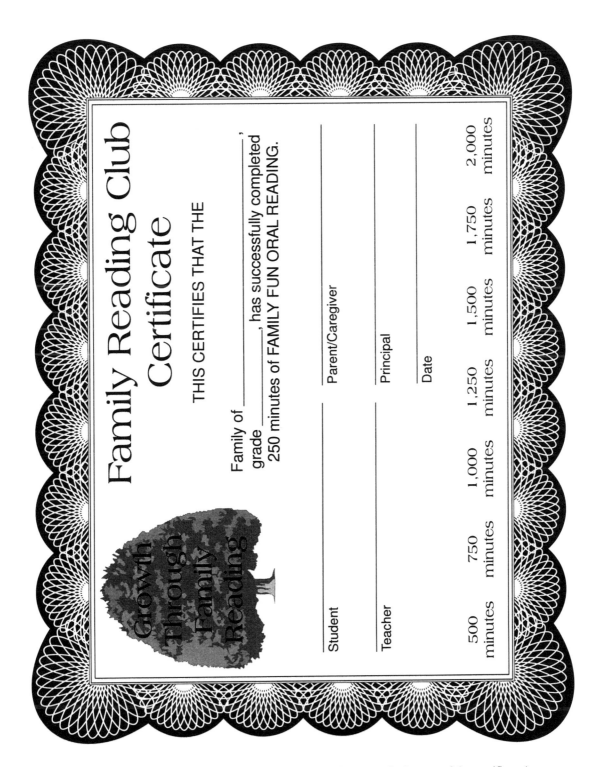

Family Reading Club Certificate

THIS CERTIFIES THAT THE

Family of _____, has successfully completed
grade _____ 250 minutes of FAMILY FUN ORAL READING.

Student _____

Teacher _____

_____ Parent/Caregiver

_____ Principal

_____ Date

Growth Through Family Reading

500 minutes	750 minutes	1,000 minutes	1,250 minutes	1,500 minutes	1,750 minutes	2,000 minutes

(**Note:** Gold stickers are placed over the number of additional minutes at the bottom of the certificate.)

Appendix III: Reading Partners Program

The second year I was principal at Garden Hills Elementary School, we began a Reading Partners program. It began because we wanted to provide additional read-aloud practice time for our students with other adults. A Title 6 representative and I brainstormed what might be workable that did not take our teachers' time or keep the students away from their classrooms for more than five minutes.

We wanted to have adult partners because we wanted our students to know that other adults beside their teachers and parents thought reading was important and cared enough to come and volunteer their time.

At first we recruited parents, but so many worked, had small children at home, and/or did not have a car. We had more teachers wanting a reading partner for their classroom than we had parent volunteers. We were able to recruit a few people from service clubs, but then we hit a gold mine . . . .

My own parents had moved to a senior citizens' home in our town. One night I attended their monthly meeting and made a request for volunteer services. We gained more reading partners than we could use. From that point, the senior citizens helped us with reading practice for our students.

Every Wednesday in October and April, the nicest months of the year for weather in Illinois, the senior citizens would come to the school (transportation was provided) for a cup of coffee. Then a PTA parent would escort them to the appropriate classrooms and they would begin their reading sessions. A PTA parent monitored the time for each session, as only five minutes of reading time was given to each student. Many senior citizens came the entire year. We welcomed their reading services anytime. The children chose their own reading material.

Many worthwhile activities resulted from this association. The senior citizens were invited to classrooms to talk about many things, we invited them to have a school lunch at a table with the children, and they had a senior hobby day. The arts and craft participants went into classrooms and made projects with the children, such as teaching the students how to knit, crochet, embroider, and tool leather. They also came and entertained classrooms with a "kitchen band," banjoes, guitars, mouth harps, etc. They taught the students games they had played as children.

The senior citizens were a big help to our school. Many times it was difficult to judge who gained the most from the meetings—the students or the senior citizens. Both were smiling and happy when the sessions ended! You as a parent could take the lead in implementing such a collaboration in your child's school (following is a sample letter to volunteers). Or, you might choose to use some of these ideas with your own child and a senior citizen whom you know. Either way, this is sure to be a rewarding experience!

Dear Reading Partner Volunteers:

The students at _____ enjoy participating in our Reading Partners program. We are continually trying to provide experiences that will motivate the students and enhance their learning environment. We believe that the school staff, the parents, the students, and other adult volunteers should work together to provide reading experiences so that the students will become better readers.

We have designated _____
(days/months)
from _____ as Reading Enrichment Days. We are
(times)
inviting parents, grandparents, senior citizens, and other interested adults to participate. We would like you to come to our school for a half hour to one hour per week to listen to students read. When you arrive, please come to the front office and tell the staff that you are there for the Reading Partners program, and they will give you a Reading Partners badge/name tag.

The main objectives of the program are to:

1. Motivate the students to read for pleasure.

2. Help the students to improve their skills by reading aloud.

3. Help the students learn to relate to adults outside their home.

4. Demonstrate to the students that other adults besides their parents think reading is important.

Please volunteer to be a Reading Partner for our students. Call the school office _____ and tell us you would like to be a
(telephone)
Reading Partner. We are looking forward to seeing you in our school at the times listed above, and all throughout the year if you wish to continue reading with our students.

Other Publications by the Author

■■■ How to Read With Your Children: Educator/Workshop Leader's Guide

The *Educator/Workshop Leader's Guide* is useful for preschool, classroom, and resource teachers; principals; librarians; or parents who would like to be a workshop leader and introduce and encourage the use of the guide by parents/caregivers either formally with a workshop group or informally on an individual basis. Included are a research-based rationale for the methodology and an outline of a three-hour training session, with reproducible handout masters for distribution to parents/caregivers.

■■■ Turning Our School Around: Seven Commonsense Steps to School Improvement

Would you like to know how a troubled school with many special needs students turned around, and in five years received the U.S. Department of Education Blue Ribbon Award for Excellence in Elementary Education? Learn how this elementary school, using common sense programs, enabled children from a diverse, multicultural, transient community to raise their reading and math scores at each grade level by three to four months in three years. Learn how the parents helped to maintain this gain by reading for 6,000 hours at home with the help of the nationally recognized Garden Hills Family Reading Club. Learn how 91-98% of the students earned "Garden Hills Number One" student recognition for exemplary behavior over a five-year period. This exciting story was written by the school's former principal, Phyllis A. Wilken.

Sopris West